THE BOOK OF
PIDGIN ENGLISH

REVISED EDITION

BY JOHN J. MURPHY

Robert Brown & Associates

BUK BILONG
TOK PISIN

First Edition 1943
Second Printing 1947
Third Printing 1949
Fourth Printing 1954
Fifth Printing 1956
Revised Edition 1959
Seventh Printing 1962
Revised Edition 1966
Revised Edition 1973
Revised Edition 1979
Eleventh Printing 1981
Revised Edition 1985

The 1985 edition designed and published by
Robert Brown & Associates (Aust) Pty. Ltd.
P.O. Box 29
Bathurst, N.S.W. 2795 Australia

© Copyright 1985

Distributed in Papua New Guinea by
Gordon & Gotch (PNG) Pty. Ltd.
P.O. Box 107,
Boroko, Papua New Guinea

ISBN 0 909197 88 1

All rights reserved. No part of this publication may be
reproduced, stored in a retrieval system or transmitted in any form or by any means, electronic, mechanical, photocopying, recording or otherwise, without
the prior permission of the publisher.

CONTENTS

FOREWORD 5
PREFACE 7
GRAMMAR
    Orthography 8
    Nouns and Pronouns 15
    Adjectives 17
    Adverbs 19
    Prepositions 22
    Verbs 23
    Miscellaneous 25
    Some Pitfalls 28
    Some Native Beliefs, Practices
       and Institutions 29
    Examples of Pidgin-English
       Composition 31
    Numerals 34
    Outline 35
CLASSIFIED VOCABULARY 55
NEO-MELANESIAN TO
ENGLISH 69
ENGLISH TO
NEO-MELANESIAN 111

Papa Deo Bilong Mipela

Papa Deo yu stap antap long Heven,
ples bilong yu:
Takondo nem bilong yu:
bai lotu na lo bilong yu i kam namil long
mipela na mipela harim tok bilong yu olsem
ol antap long Heven i harim na bihainim:
Mekim kamap gut abus bilong mipela
long wok na long bus:
larim mipela long ol pekato,
Papa, olsem mipela i marimari
long husat ol i mekim pasin
nogut long mipela:
Papa yu no ken traim tumas
mipela taronggu; tasol pulim bek
na sambai long mipela sapos
samting nogut laik krongutim mipela.
Heven i bilong yu wanpela tasol
na strong na bilas bilong yu i noken lus;
stap oltaim, oltaim tasol.

                                        Amen.

FOREWORD

Captain John J. Murphy has asked me to write a foreword to "The Book of Pidgin English".

When Civil Administration ceased in New Guinea early in 1942, that fine body of men who belonged to the field staffs of the Territories was absorbed into the Australian New Guinea Administrative Unit. Captain Murphy was one of these and has latterly performed sterling and gallant service in the immediate vicinity of the enemy.

As a newcomer to the land where Pidgin English is spoken I find Captain Murphy's book intensely interesting. He shows by examples the adaptability of the language (who else would have thought of rendering one of Shakespeare's choicest morsels in Pidgin!), and wisely warns the beginner of the difference between true Pidgin English and "broken" English.

The book might be regarded as a standard work upon what has been a most controversial subject, and it forms a useful guide for those dealing with natives in the areas where Pidgin English is the lingua franca.

I have been informed by others that the labour involved in collecting material for the book has, over many years, occupied the all too few spare hours of a conscientious Patrol Officer. No doubt for Captain Murphy it was a labour of love, yet any success that the book achieves will be richly deserved.

I wish Captain Murphy and his book the best of luck.

Port Moresby,
September 1943

BASIL MORRIS,
Major-General,
G.O.C. ANGAU.

PREFACE

This book is recast in the standard orthography, as determined by the Department of Education in New Guinea after a long period of research. Eminent linguists outside New Guinea were engaged.

Back in 1941, in my Preface to the First Edition, I said, hopefully: "Hence this book, which was undertaken as a step towards the classification of Melanesian Pidgin English and its reduction to measureable and grammatical terms; also to stimulate, perhaps, worthier and more competent lexicographers to undertake the task of stabilizing the most widely (numerically and geographically) spoken language in the Territory of New Guinea."

This almost wistful hope was expressed at a time when it was not far short of a lone voice – when the language was belittled; accepted, in most cases, with tolerant amusement as O.K. for third or fourth class citizens and even vehemently called a "horror of horrors". After the War, cultural hermits cried the slogan, "Out Base Varlet!"

At the invitation of the Department of Education a world distinguished linguist arrived to look at Pidgin English. He was Professor Robert Hall, Jr., from Cornell University. He delivered a most hearty thump to the detractors in his "Hands Off Pidgin" – the People's Language. In 1956 the Department of Education published "The Standard Neo-Melanesian (Pidgin) Orthography". This set the spelling for what up to that time was at the mercy of individuals. Pidgin English is respectable!

In the meantime learned scholars like the Reverend Father Francis Mihalic, S.V.D., and Reverend Dr L.J. Luzbetak, of the Mission of the Holy Ghost at Alexishaven, have contributed works that exceed in depth and learning most other works on the World's "Marginal Languages".

As far away as Brazil a learned judge and most versatile scholar, Judge Newton Sabba Guimaraes, writes penetratingly and affectionately about Melanesian Pidgin English.

Father Mihalic still laments, however, "though there are 200 linguists painstakingly putting fifty languages down on paper, not one of them is specialising in the Universal vernacular, Pidgin."

Yes, Pidgin English has come a long way. It is an official language in the House of Assembly; a recognised foreign language in the Queensland University Institute of Modern Languages and at the Port Moresby University; the Gospels and the Bible are translated into Pidgin English; liturgy too; Primers, text books, readers; magazines and two newspapers; six broadcasting stations use it daily.

And my wistful hope? It is realised.

GRAMMAR

I

ORTHOGRAPHY

The inconsistencies of the English system render it an unsatisfactory medium for representing the sounds of Melanesian Pidgin-English.

In 1956 the Minister for Territories approved an official Neo-Melanesian Orthography to be standard in all fields in which Pidgin is used in the Territory of Papua-New Guinea.

An exact phonemic analysis of Neo-Melanesian used over the Territory has been made and an Orthograpy devised for it by Dr R.A. Hall, Jnr., Professor of Modern Languages at Cornell University[1].

The orthography is the phonemic orthography determined by Dr Hall, modified by three extrinsic non-linguistic factors:

(1) Cultural pressure. This is seen as a strong opposition to any letters, diacritics, or other usages which are not standard English practice, particularly Australian and British English practice.

(2) Selection of one dialect. Dr Hall has described Neo-Melanesian as it is spoken over the whole of New Guinea, by both native and non-native speakers. His is therefore the most complete description, and takes into account all the phonemes used in a wide range of dialects, including those phonemes not normally used by native speakers.

With the criterion of the teaching of reading and writing as paramount, the linguistically accurate orthography of Dr Hall has been modified to a less-than-linguistically-accurate sub-phonemic orthography, based on Dr Hall's findings, but with the emphasis centred on one particular dialect – that spoken by rather older Melanesian speakers at Madang – rather than on the complete Neo-Melanesian of the Territory.

(3) Practical school experience. Objective and practical norms constituted the main criteria, so that at times theory had to give way to practical expedients. The dialects of Neo-Melanesian spoken by non-native speakers have been excluded from the data serving as a basis for the orthography, resulting in a reduction in the total number of phonemes which have to be considered for orthographical purposes. It is desired to spread literacy as quickly

---

[1]. A Standard Orthography and List of Spellings for Neo-Melanesian (Department of Education, Port Moresby, 1955).

and efficiently as possible, and an orthography which is easier for the native is preferred to one which, although providing for all the phonemes for all dialects, may use several letters not needed in particular dialects. These differences of dialect in Neo-Melanesian cause difficulties in the preparation of an overall orthography, and accordingly at the meeting of the Committee on Languages in February, 1955, the particular dialect spoken at Madang was selected as the standard. Madang was chosen for its central position geographically in the Neo-Melanesian area, and because it represented a Neo-Melanesian as unaffected as possibly by the introduction of English. These considerations and not any preference for any existing orthography have determined the final choice of letters.

The Alphabet

There are twenty-two letters in the alphabet.

Letter	Pronunciation	Letter	Pronunciation
a	ah	m	em
b	bay	n	en
d	day	o	or, o
e	as in "pen"	p	pay
f	eff	r	er
g	gay never at end of word except words ending in NG: use K	s	ess
h	ha	t	tay
i	ee	u	as in "put"
j	jay	v	vay
k	kay	w	wee
l	ell	y	yee begins word only

It will be noticed that C, Q, X, and Z of the English alphabet have been omitted. Their place is taken by K, or S, KW, KIS, S respectively.

It is important to know the sounds of the vowels and the diphthongs.

Vowels –

A	=	ah; as in "man"	O	=	or; as in "hot"
E	=	as in "pen"	U	=	as in "put"
I	=	ee; as in "hit"			

Diphthongs

There are three diphthongs, *Viz.*-

AI – almost identical with the sound of the English letter "i".
AU – almost identical with the sound of "ow" in "how".
OI – as in "boil".

The combination IU is often used to denote the long "u" as in "rude". After "s", the "I" of "IU" takes on the function of an "h"; and so we spell the Pidgin-English word meaning "to shoot" as SIUTIM.

*Anglicisms**

Anglicisms in orthography, if allowed to creep in, will cause great and needless trouble to natives who know no English. In particular, the English letters *C*, *qu* and *x* are useless even in English spelling; their presence is a defect of our spelling system, and their introduction does nothing but render that of Neo-Melanesian inconsistent and confusing. To write such a word as "council", use the spelling *Kaunsil;* for "queen", write *Kwin;* for "axe", Neo-Melanesian uses *Akis*.

If it is necessary to give English spellings, for example to enable readers to recognize words on labels or signs, give first the consistent spelling in terms of Neo-Melanesian orthography, and then the English spelling in parentheses: e.g. *Kidni* (kidney); *Bensin* (benzine).

One is often tempted to believe that the wholesale introduction of English spellings into Neo-Melanesian orthography will facilitate the later learning of English, or bring Neo-Melanesian closer to English. In fact, however, they serve only to disorient the speaker of Neo-Melanesian; the complexities of English orthography should be left until the learner already has some acquaintance with English as it is spoken. Much of the difficulty of our present-day English spelling was caused by Renaissance scholars who introduced Latinising fashions of writing words, under the delusion that they were "ennobling" the language.

The widespread belief that it is possible gradually to turn Neo-Melanesian into English by the introduction of English words takes no account of the fact that the vocabulary represents only one part of the language. The grammatical structure and phonetics still remain those of Neo-Melanesian, and at best the result could never be more than another Pidgin. The belief is not only wrong but dangerous, as by introducing English into Neo-Melanesian in this way, the native finally reaches a confusion point, where he does not know whether he is speaking Neo-Melanesian or English.

This does not mean that Neo-Melanesian cannot be used for the teaching of English – on the contrary, it is one of the most valuable aids in this Territory for this purpose. But it cannot be done by introducing English as is currently done in the *Rabaul News* and on the Native People's Session. (These two media have so much English introduced that surveys taken in 1953 and again in 1956 show that the English-loaded Neo-Melanesian they use is very difficult to understand outside the Rabaul area.)

---

* The Standard Neo-Melanesian (Pidgin) Orthography (Department of Education, Port Moresby, 1956).

Variations in Pronunciation

Variations in pronunciation are apt to induce some variations in spelling, as follows:

Many Melanesians have difficulty pronouncing groups of consonant sounds, especially at the beginning of words, as in *St-, sp-, sk, pr-, br-, fr-, tr-, dr-, kr-, gr-, pl-, bl-, fl-, kl-, gl-*. In pronunciation, they often insert an extra vowel between consonants: thus *Stap* "be located" will often sound like *Sitap* or *satap*; *Flai* "fly" like *filai, pilai*, etc., and will often spell the words accordingly. Such spellings are not to be recommended, however, for three reasons: (a) this extra vowel is not phonemically significant, since its presence or absence makes no difference to the meaning of the word involved; (b) it is not constant, varying from *I* to *a* according to the region and the speaker; (c) an increasing number of speakers are learning to pronounce the consonant combinations without the extra vowel. To write the vowel under these circumstances is to use a naive phonetic transcription rather than a sound phonemically-based orthography. We will, therefore, write *Stap, flai*, etc. Exceptions: *ks* at the end of a word, e.g. Bokis, Akis and *ns*, e.g. Banis.

In many Melanesian languages, the sounds *B, d,* and *g* have their onset strongly nasalised, making them sound to European ears like *Mb, nd,* and *ngg*: thus *buk* "book" may be pronounced like *mbuk*; *dai* "cease, stop" like *ndai*; or *go* "go" like *nggo*. In some words, especially in the interior of the word between vowels, the pronunciation *mb, nd,* or *ngg* has become permanent in the usage of both Melanesians and Europeans, and we will write it as such: e.g. *tambu* "prohibition"; "forbidden". In other instances, especially at the beginning of words, usage varies and the constant element is the *b-, d-* or *g-* sound; hence we will not mark the pre-nasalisation in writing.

Word-Boundaries

We are often tempted to write Neo-Melanesian words separately or together in accordance with our spelling of the related words in English: e.g. *kam ap* "arrive" (Eng. *come up), bik fela* "big" (Eng. *big fellow),* or *bring im* "bring (transitive)" (Eng. *bring him).* Such a procedure imposes on Neo-Melanesian the structure of an alien language and fails to take into account the way that Neo-Melanesian itself functions. In Neo-Melanesian, the division between words is determined by stress, each new word having a fresh stress on its first syllable (phonemically speaking, and disregarding the extra inserted vowels in consonant clusters). We will, therefore, write as one word all syllables following a stressed syllable: *kamap, bikfela, bringim.*

An exception to the principle just stated is found in the unstressed syllable *i,* which occurs before predicates, normally after all subjects except *mi* "I", *mipela* "we", *yu* "you", *yupela* "you(pl.)", and *yumi* "you and I"; *i* also occurs in subjectless sentences. For instance; *dispela man i-go* "this man goes"; *em i-go* "he goes"; *dispela haus i-bikpela* "this house is large"; *mi tripela i-kamap* "the three of us arrive"; *i-ren* "it rains". This syllable, though unstressed, belongs with the elements following it; its grammatical function is that of a "predicate-marker", telling the hearer that what follows is the predicate of the clause. (It is acceptable to write it without a hyphen: *dispela man i go, em i go, mi tripela i kamap, i ren.*) However, such spellings as *emi go* "he goes" or *oli go* "they go", with the *i* attached to the preceding pronoun, show a fundamental misunderstanding of the grammatical function of *i* (there are no such pronoun forms as *emi* or *oli!*) and are therefore to be avoided.

Particular Spellings

The following cases warrant specific attention:

(1) *p* and *f*. The occurrence of *p* and *f* in Neo-Melanesian is of two kinds:
   (i) Words always pronounced with *p* and *f* are written as such e.g. *paip* "pipe"; *faiv* "five".
   (ii) Words in which *p* or *f* are interchanged. In this case *p* should be used. (There will be comparatively few occurrences of *f*.)

(2) *Final r*. This is written when it is pronounced by a *native*, e.g. *kar* "car", *star* "star", *bruder* "Mission Brother". Where it is not pronounced by a *native* it should not be written, e.g. *mo, moa* "more", *tisa* "teacher", *dua* "door", *klia* "clear". (Not *mor, tisar, tiser, dor,* or *klir.*)

(3) *s*. This letter includes, besides *s* itself, the following sounds, all of which are heard occasionally but are exceptional pronunciations:
   ch. e.g. *ticha*, which will be written *tisa*.
   sh. e.g. *shoim*, which will be written *soim*.
   j. e.g. *kabij*, which will be written *kabis*.
   [Note that in a few words where this sound occurs *initially*, the letter *j* is retained, e.g. *Jun* "June".]
   ts. Only in those cases where an attempt is being made to copy the *ch* of English.
   e.g., *titsa*, which will be spelt *tisa*.
   [But words like *wetsan* remain as such.]

(4) *ng* as in "singer" is so spelt (e.g., MANGAL), but becomes *ngg* as the sound in "finger" (e.g., MANGGO). Several words which are at

present spelt everywhere by using *nk* for *ngk* will be left unchanged, due to strong pressure of opinion. They constitute only a small group which can be learned as sight words.

e.g. ink (ingk); manki (mangki); bank (bangk); blanket (blangket); drink (dringk); aitink (aitingk).

(5) The consonants *b*, *d* and *g* are not voiced at the ends of words, and so will be written *p*, *t* and *k*.

e.g. *p*: *rap* "rub", *krip* "crib"
t: *gut* "good", *hait* "hide"
k: *bik* "big"

(6) Consonant clusters at the ends of words drop the final consonant, e.g. *ailan* "island". (Where the final consonant does occur, it is because the native is attempting to imitate English.)

(7) *bilong, sapos*. Both of these words belong to a group in which the first syllable is stressed as often or more often than the second. They will, therefore, be written as above, and not *blong, spos*.

(8) *w* and *y*. Some writers of Neo-Melanesian have omitted both *w* and *y*, and used in their place *u* and *i*, in the belief that they were effecting an economy in the orthography. Where these sounds occur, study of the pattern of consonants and vowels in the language must be made, to determine in each case whether the *w* and *y* are necessary. The choice is not an arbitrary one. In English and in Neo-Melanesian the consonant-vowel pattern determines that *w* and *y* are necessary, as well as *u* and *i*. In other languages, only *u* and *i* are necessary.

(9) As mentioned earlier [para. 3.(3)], the dialect spoken at Madang will be regarded as the standard. Queries as to spelling should be referred to that area, taking care to allow for differences of pronunciation even within that area.

This orthography should not influence the pronunciation of Neo-Melanesian in any way. The differences in speech in various areas will continue, as the standard orthography is an attempt to provide uniformity in writing and not to interfere with spoken Neo-Melanesian.

II

NOUNS AND PRONOUNS

Nouns

Singular and Plural – The singular form of the noun suffers no change in form for the plural. The *number* of a noun is inferred from its nature, its qualifying adjectives and the text.

Articles – Inflection, context and qualifying adjectives take their place. If precision is desired, WANPELA (one) is used for the indefinite article, and "the" is represented by HIA (this).

Examples-
(a) TASOL DOK HIA NO LUKIM WANPELA MAN I SINDAUN LONG NAMBIS.
    But the dog did not see a man sitting on the beach.

(b) EM I KRAI OLSEM PISIN.
    He called like a bird.

(c) MI SAVE SIUTIM BALUS.
    I can shoot pigeons.

(d) MI HARIM BALUS I KRAI. I STAP WE?
    I heard a pigeon. Where is he?

(e) PLES I NO GAT MAN.
    There are no men in the village.

(f) IM I MAN BILONG SINGSING TRU.
    He is a man fond of parties.

Case – The form for all the cases is the same. The noun suffers no change of form or ending.

Gender – In Pidgin-English as in English, gender depends on the presence or absence of sex. Adjectives meaning "male" and "female" are MAN and MERI respectively; e.g. DOK MERI is a female dog and a male infant is a PIKININI MAN.

Abstract Nouns – There are quite a number of abstract nouns. To name but a few SAVE (sagacity), DAI (death), KRANKI (foolishness), WOK (duty), PRET (fear), LAIK (desire) and many others.

Pronouns

Personal Pronouns

Person	Singular	Dual	Plural
1st	MI	YUMI	MIPELA
2nd	YU	–	YUPELA
3rd	EM	–	OL

YUMI is also used by a person speaking within a group and identifying himself with the group:
>YUMI NO SAVE KAIKAI KUNAI.
>We (you and I) don't eat grass.

MIPELA is used to a third person outside a group with which the speaker identifies himself, but does not include the person addressed:
>MIPELA NO LUKIM DOK BILONG YU.
>We (my friends and I) didn't see your dog.

Demonstrative Pronouns – There are no Demonstrative Pronouns. A Demonstrative Adjective with a noun is used instead (vide Demonstrative Adjectives).

Interrogative Pronouns – Who and whom are translated by HUSAT.
>HUSAT I KAM?
>Who is coming?
>LUKIM HUSAT?
>Whom did you see?

Whose is translated by BILONG HUSAT.
>BUK BILONG HUSAT?
>Whose book is this?

What is translated by WONEM?
>YU MEKIM WONEM?
>What are you doing?

Which is translated by HUSAT or by WONEM, according as it is used for a person or for a thing. Sometimes it is translated by a noun and an Interrogative Adjective-
>WONEM MAN I TOK TRU?
>Which (of them) is telling the truth?

Relative Pronouns

Who is translated by HUSAT.
AI BILONG YU LUKIM HUSAT I MEKIM?
Did you actually see who did it?
Whom is omitted or circumvented.
EM DISPELA MAN YU LUKIM EM LONG ROT?
Is this the man (whom) you saw on the road?
Whose and *Which* are treated in the same way.
YU SAVE DISPELA KIAP, GRAS BILONGEM I WET?
Do you know this Kiap (whose) hair is white?

III

ADJECTIVES

Proper – The proper Noun is used as a Proper Adjective.
EM I *SEPIK*.
He is a Sepik (man).

Quantitive-
EM I GAT *PLANTI* MONI.
He has *much* money.
LIKLIK DOK HIA EM I KAIKAI PIG *OLGETA*.
This little dog ate the *whole* pig.
MI KAIKAI *LIKLIK* RAIS PASTAIM.
Let me have a *little* rice to eat.

N.B. – In this instance OLGETA follows the noun. Preceding the noun it means "all of the ....'s."

Few may be translated by the phrase – I NO PLANTI.
Other Quantitive Adjectives are rendered by nouns.

Cardinal Numeral-

One	wanpela	Six	sikispela
Two	tupela	Seven	sevenpela
Three	tripela	Eight	etpela
Four	foapela	Nine	nainpela
Five	faipela	Ten	tenpela

Eleven – wanpela ten wan; etc.
Twenty – tupelaten; Thirty – tripelaten; etc.

Ordinal Numeral –

First	namba wan	Sixth	namba sikis
Second	namba tu	Seventh	namba seven
Third	namba tri	Eighth	namba et
Fourth	namba foa	Ninth	namba nain
Fifth	namba faiv	Tenth	namba ten

Indefinite Numerals – They are OLGETA, OL (all), PLANTI (many). *Few* may be translated by the phrase – I NO PLANTI.

MI SIUTIM *OLGETA* PIK.
I shot *all* the pigs.
WESTAP *OL* MAN?
Where are *all* the men?
PLANTI MAN I *NO GAT* MERI.
Many men *have no* wives.
MI LUKIM SAMPELA MAN, TASOL *I NO PLANTI*.
I saw *some* men, but only *a few*.

Demonstrative Adjectives – This, that, these and those are translated by HIA, EM ... HIA, DISPELA.

DOK *HIA* NO GAT TIS.
EM DOK *HIA* I NO GAT TIS.
DISPELA DOK I NO GAT TIS.
This dog has no teeth.

The context indicates whether This or That, These or Those is meant, but *dispela* is always singular.

Indefinite Demonstrative – Such, Other, Same.

MAN *OLSEM* I NOKEN LULUAI.
Such a man cannot be a Luluai.
PUTIM *ARAPELA* BOKIS ANANIT.
Put the *other* box underneath.
MI SOIMAPIM LAPLAP BILONG MI. YU MEKIM *OLSEM* BILONG YU.
I will sew my lavalava. You do the *same* (thing) to yours.

Another is translated by NARAPELA.

Interrogative Adjectives – Which and What are translated by WONEM.

WONEM MAN?
Which man?

WONEM KAIKAI?
What food?

Distributive Adjectives – They are circumvented by phrase or construction. But Every may be translated by OLGETA.
OLGETA MAN I HOLIM SPIA.
Every man held a spear.

Comparison of Adjectives

The comparison of Adjectives is, as a rule, regular. Emphasis and voice inflection are sometimes used. There are two classes of regular comparison – the class which is compared like LIKLIK and the class which is compared like HANGGRE.

Positive	Comparative	Superlative
Liklik	liklik moa	liklik long ol (smallest)
		liklik tumas (very small)
Strongpela	strongpela moa	strongpela long ol (strongest)
		strongpela tumas (very strong)
Gutpela	gutpela moa	winim ol (best)
		gutpela tumas (very good)
Hanggre	hanggre moa	hanggre tumas
Planti	planti moa	planti tumas

Adjectives describing qualities, dispositions and characteristics are compared like LIKLIK. All others are compared like HANGGRE.

IV

ADVERBS

Almost any Adjective is capable of being used, without any change of form, as an Adverb. There is a class of Adjective, however, ending in –PELA, which drops the ending when used as an Adverb.
1. EM I *STRONGPELA* MAN, SAVE WOK *STRONG*.
2. *GUTPELA* MAN HIA, SAVE HARIM *GUT* TOK BILONG LULUAI.
1. He is a *strong* man and will work *diligently*.
2. This is a *good* man. He heeds *well* what his Luluai says.

Simple Adverbs – Adverbs of Manner and of Degree are straightforward.

> EM I MEKIM *OLSEM*.
> He acted *thus*.
> *KLOSAP* I PUNDAUN.
> He *almost* fell over.

Number-

> *OLTAIM* EM I LES TASOL.
> He is *always* loafing.
> MI KAM *GEN* LONG PIKUS.
> I came *again* to the fig tree.

Time-

> LONGTAIM *BIPO*.
> A long time *ago*.
> *BIPOTAIM* YU MEKIM OLSEM.
> You did this same thing *before*.

Place-

> PUTIM LONG *HAP, KLOSTU* LONG DUA.
> Put it over *there, near* the door.
> MI STAP *NISAIT*.
> I remained *inside*.

Probability-

> Translated by AITINGK. But see p.46.
> *AITING* DOK I KAIKAI.
> *Probably* a dog ate it.

Interrogative Adverbs

Manner-

> YU KAM *OLSEM WONEM?*
> *How* did you come?

Cause-

> YU KAM *BILONG* WONEM?
> *Why* did you come?

But censoriously-

> *BILONG WONEM* YU KAM?

Why is translated in several ways-
> BILONG WONEM
> HAUSAT
> WASAMARA
> WATPO

HAUSAT and WASAMARA are used emphatically. WATPO is most often used rhetorically:
> *WATPO* YUMI HADWOK TUMAS? PE I LIKLIK TASOL.
> *Why* should we travail? We only get a small pay.
> *HAUSAT* YU NO KAM?
> *Why* did you not come?

WATPO is also used censoriously:
> *WATPO* YU NO PAINIM GUT?
> *Why* didn't you make a good search?

Time-
> YU KAM LONG *WONEM TAIM?*
> *When* did you come?

Number-
> *HAUMAS TAIM* YU KAM?
> *How often* did you come?
> N.B. - What is the time? - HAUMAS KLOK?

Place-
> YU KAM *WE?*
> *From where* did you come?
> YU GO *WE?*
> *Where* are you going?

Relative or Conjunctive Adverbs-

YU SAVE LONG *WONEM TAIM* EM I MEKIM?
Do you know *when* he did it?
YU SAVE *OLSEM WONEM* EMI I KAM?
Do you know *how* he came?
YU SAVE *BILONG WONEM* EM I KAM?
Do you know why he came?
YU SAVE EM I KAM *WE?*
Do you know *whence* he came?

Comparison -
Having the same form as the corresponding Adjective, Adverbs are compared in the same manner as the Adjectives.

V

PREPOSITIONS

There are only two prepositions but they cover the whole range of English translations, either by themselves, or in combination with a phrase. They are LONG and BILONG.

Into, Through, Under, Inside, In are translated by NISAIT LONG.

LONG covers In, By, On, With, From, To, At.
BILONG covers For and Of.
> MI GO *LONG* ROT *LONG* MANDE *LONG* SALAMAUA NA SIUTIM BALUS *LONG* BUNARA *BILONG* BRATA *BILONG* ME, *BILONG* KAIKAI.
> I went *by* road *on* Monday *to* Salamaua and shot a pigeon *with* the bow *of* the brother *of* me, *for* food.

BILONG also means "for the purpose of", "because", "in order to", e.g.:
> EM I KATIM KANDA *BILONG* PAITIM YUPELA.
> He is cutting a cane *for the purpose of* beating you.
> EM I KRAI *BILONG* KIAP I PAITIM.
> He is crying *because* the Kiap beat him.
> EM I KAM *BILONG* HARIM TOK.
> He came *in order to* hear the news.

LONG is also sometimes used as a conjunction.
> EM I WET *LONG* PAPA I PINISTAIM.
> He is waiting *until* his father has finished his contract of service.

If is translated by SAPOS, as well as by TASOL.
> YU KEN GO *SAPOS* YU WOK GUT.
> You may go *if* you work well.
> YU NOKEN WOK LONG ME *SAPOS* YU *NO* SAVE KUK.
> You cannot work for me *unless* you can cook (*if* you can *not* cook).
> N.B. – SAPOS... NO. = Unless.
> *TASOL* EM I KAM, MI KEN HASKIM EM.
> *If* he had come, I could have asked him.

VI

VERBS

Verbs in Pidgin-English are very simply conjugated and suffer a minimum of form change. Context and inflection generally distinguish between the tenses. There is no Passive Voice. The English Passive is directly translated into the Active or rendered by an Adjective. Past Participles are treated as Adjectives.

There are Transitive, Intransitive and Auxiliary verbs of which the Indicative only is conjugated, and that very simply. The Subjunctive Mood is inferred.

Most Transitive verbs are distinguished by the fact that they end in – IM. Frequently an Intransitive verb is made Transitive by adding –IM.

WOK .... WOKIM
RON .... RONIM
SANAP .... SANAPIM

But-
LUKLUK .... LUKIM
TOKTOK .... TOKIM

A few verbs are both Transitive and Intransitive, e.g. KAIKAI.

The Verb "To Be".

(1) In its auxiliary sense the predicate marker, I, is used; OL *I* KAM NAU – they *are* coming now.
(2) In its sense of state of being or presence; YU *STAP* WE? where *are* you?; EM *I STAP* KAIKAI – he is eating; MI *STAP* GUT nd I *am* well.
(3) In its indicative sense, the transitive verb "to have", with predicate marker, I, hops in to give a hand; *I GAT* PLANTI MAN I *STAP* – there are plenty of men.

Conjugations – Conjunctions are regular and simple.

Only the Indicative Mood is conjugated. There is no change in the verb in the tenses – one form suffices for each tense for the singular and plural of all persons.

All Present Tenses

Person	Singular	Plural
1st	Go	Go
2nd	Go	Go
3rd	Go	Go

Past Perfect Tense

	Singular	Plural
1st	Go pinis Bin go	Go pinis Bin go
2nd	Go pinis Bin go	Go pinis Bin go
3rd	Go pinis Bin go	Go pinis Bin go

These are really the only tenses. All other tenses, including the future, are implied or inferred. But if the immediate future is meant, i.e. "about to", it is conjugated thus:

1st Person	Laik go	bai mi go
2nd Person	Laik go	bai yu go
3rd Person	Laik go	bai em i go

Auxiliary Verbs – There are only two Auxiliary Verbs – BIN and LAIK. BIN forms the Past Perfect Indicative Mood. LAIK forms the Immediate Future, but it must be distinguished from the Transitive Verb meaning "desire" or "wish". In this latter case it is generally followed by "I". The context also helps in distinguishing the one from the other. (See also Sub-para. (1) above.)

BALUS *I LAIK* GO NAU.
The aeroplane is *about* to go.
EM *I LAIK* I GO LONG BALUS.
He *wishes* to travel by aeroplane.

There are some verbs which are Passive in *sense*, but Active in *form*:

MI FILIM *NOGUT*.
I do not feel *well*.
SUSU I SMEL *NOGUT*.
The milk smells *sour*.

VII

MISCELLANEOUS

Inflection – Inflection forms a very important part of Melanesian Pidgin-English. It not only has the more obvious function of marking interrogation, but also often determines the meaning of words, the case and number of nouns, the tenses of verbs, and, in fact, supplies a deal of the desiderata of Pidgin-English. The use and function of inflection can be learned best by experience.

Order of Words – There is a general resemblance to the order of words in English, but often a word depends for its meaning on its position in the sentence. Consequently the order of words is important.

(a) MI *TASOL* I GO LONG KAIKAI.
Only I went to eat.
(b) MI GO LONG *TASOL* KAIKAI.
I went *only* to eat.
(c) MI GO LONG KAIKAI *TASOL*.
I *only* went to eat.
(d) *TASOL* MI GO LONG KAIKAI.
But I went to eat.
(e) IM I LUKIM *TASOL* MI.
He saw *only* me.

It must be said, however, that (b) and (e) are rare. The general practice in this case is to have TASOL follow the word it qualifies and place the emphasis on that word.

In statements, Adverbs of Time precede the subject and verb.
ASDE MI LUKIM YU.
I saw you *yesterday*.

But in question, if the Adverb is stressed or emphasised above the verb, the Adverb goes first. If the verb is stressed, then it goes first.
MI *LUKIM* YU ASDE?
Did I *see* you yesterday?
ASDE MI LUKIM YU?
Did I see you *yesterday*?

There is an exception to the rule for statements when a preposition is used to form an Adverbial Phrase.
> OL I MEKIM *LONG* BIPO.
> They made them *in the past*; or
> They *used* to make them.

Adverbs of Place follow the sentence in statement and in question.
> PUTIM LONG *HAP*.
> Put it over *there*.
> PUTIM LONG *HAP*?
> Shall I put it over *there*?
> MI LAIK I SINDAUN *NISAIT*.
> I would like to sit *inside*.
> YU GO *WE*?
> *Where* are you going?
> PAUS BILONG ME STAP *WE*?
> *Where* is my suitcase?

The Adverb WESTAP goes first, however:
> OLGETA MAN STAP *WE*?
> *WESTAP* OL MAN?
> *Where* is everybody?

Adverbs of Manner follow:
> IM I WOKABAUT *STRONG*.
> He walks *vigorously*.
> MEKIM *OLSEM WONEM*?
> *How* did you do it?

However, in the Imperative, the Adverb goes first:
> STRONG I GO!
See also Adverbs of Cause – Why.

When MEKIM is used, meaning "to cause", it is followed immediately by the Infinitive:
> MI *MEKIM* SAVE YU!
> I'll *teach* you!
> KAIP *MEKIM DAI* PIK.
> The Kiap *killed* the pig.

Nating – Many English words beginning with "un" can be translated by "nating". The word means "to lack", "be without", "un-accoutred", "vacant", "unmarked", "of no account", etc. The preceding question or statement fixes the meaning of "nating".

> Examples:
> EM I NO KARIM RUKSAK; EM I KAM *NATING*.
> He didn't bring a rucksack; he came *without*.
> MI NO ASKIM; I GIPIM MI *NATING*.
> I didn't ask for it; he gave it to me *unasked* (or of his own accord).
> YU LAIK KAIKAI PASTAIM? NOGAT, MI GO *NATING*.
> Would you like to eat first? No. I'll go *without eating*.
> NO KESIM PE: MIPELA WOK *NATING*.
> We got no pay; we worked *for nothing*.
> EM I NO KARIM MASKET: EM I GO *NATING*.
> He did not have a rifle; he went *unarmed*.
> NO, MI NO TOK; MI SINDAUN *NATING*.
> No, I did not speak; I *just* sat there.
> YU *SAMTING NATING*.
> You are *of no account*.
> YU GAT PLET? NOGAT MI KAIKAI *NATING*.
> Have you a plate? No, I eat *without one*.
> EM I KALABUS *NATING*.
> He was *wrongfully* imprisoned.
> LONGPELA *NATING*.
> Long *and thin*.
> MI TOK *NATING*.
> I surmise. I speak *suppositionally*.

Gen – This adverb usually means "again" or "once more", but there is a more obscure meaning, *viz.,* "despise it", "notwithstanding", "nevertheless".

> EM I SOIM MI, TASOL MI LONGLONG *GEN*.
> He showed me, but I got mixed up *nevertheless*.

Klosap and Klostu – These two are frequently confused. Klosap never means "near to". Klostu never means "nearly".

> KLOSAP mi pundaun KLOSTU long bokis.
> I *nearly* fell over *near* the box.

VIII

SOME PITFALLS

PLE – Besides meaning "to joke", "to chaff", "play a game", etc., PLE also means, generally in reference to male with female, "to have sexual intercourse". If you say TUPELI I PLE and you refer to a man and a girl, the only meaning is "they had sexual intercourse". But TUPELA I PLE TENIS (or KRIKET, etc.) will save you from an accusation of calumny. TOK PLE means to joke or chaff.

BOKIS – In addition to its common meaning, BOKIS is also a polite term for the vagina. If you are referring to a suitcase or a trunk belonging to a woman don't say "BOKIS BILONG MISIS". Similarly, a woman will not refer to "BOKIS BILONG MI". A man can refer to "BOKIS BILONG MI" or "BOKIS BILONG MASTA" with impunity. If you speak of a woman's suitcase, etc., use PAUS, KEIS. (See TOK BOKIS.)

TOK BOKIS – Appears in general terms in the vocabulary. It is hard to keep abreast of as fashions in TOK BOKIS come and go. It is often insulting and provocative. A few examples from my time are as follows:

Oh nainsi, mi dai long yu yet! This was called out from a group at a passing Beau Brummel. Literally it is an expression of love and desire for a young lady, but here it means – "Oh you big poofter, I could go for you!"

Goan, givim buai long em. A kindly thought you would think, but, in the right place, it means – "Go and give that galah a thump".

Wo! Manuwa i kam. – "Get a load of the fat bloke."
Gras bilong lek! – "Hundreds of 'em!"

PUSIM – This word has only one meaning, *i.e.*, "to copulate with". It does not mean "to push". SIUBIM is the word meaning "to push" or "to shove". You will not, therefore, when requiring a shove, invite or command a person to PUSIM MI.

KILIM – Does not mean to "kill", though it may result in death. It means "to strike" or "to hit hard". KILIMI I DAI will translate "kill".

SELIM – Means "to send" and not "to sell", though payment may be expected after sending. "To sell" is translated by PEIM.

PEIM – Does not mean to pay (see above). The word "to pay" is BAIM which also means "to buy".

N.B. – There are no such words as: Whysat, gotim, wantim, tellim, broke, broke'im, callim (meaning to call), cryout.
If you tell your boy to WOKIM TEBOL, don't be annoyed if he takes hammer and saw and begins to make a table. He probably wouldn't know you wanted him to LAINIM TEBOL (i.e. set the table). To clear the table is TEKEWE, not RAUSIM.

Distinguish between MEKIM and WOKIM. The former means "to do" and the latter "to make", or "to cause".

SISA and BRATA may occasion confusion at first (see dictionary). A woman's sister is her BRATA and her brother is her SISA. On the other hand, a man's brother is his BRATA and his sister his SISA. The terms reach further than this, for they also include cousins. Cousins of the same sex are BRATA, of different sex – SISA.

KANDERE is a maternal uncle and he calls his sister's sons and daughters KANDERE also. It used to be spelt in a variety of ways – most popular seems to have been KANTIRI. But under no circumstance does it mean "country". Other uncles are PAPA – same as father, because that's how they are regarded, or SMOLPAPA if you want to be specific.

DAI also means "to faint", "to fall into a deep sleep" or become "hypnotised or anaesthetised". It does not conclusively mean "to die".

IX

SOME NATIVE BELIEFS, PRACTICES AND INSTITUTIONS

Gift Exchange – Previously, except on specific trading occasions, buying and selling did not exist. A gift is made, but it is incumbent on the recipient to return one of equal or greater value. This return is expected. Through contact with the European, however, the system is being modified, as a cash economy is supplanting the old customs. Native law and custom sanction this gift exchange, and, if reciprocation is not made within a reasonable time, the donor considers himself defrauded. A native, therefore, cannot deny a debt on the plea that what he received was a gift, even though he claims that he did not ask for it. He is merely trying to convert both systems – European and Native – to his own advantage.

A boil, Bubo or swelling in the groin was formerly at any rate, ascribed to walking over a spot where someone has recently micturated.

MUN and SANDE – It is the practice among many labourers to form groups and pool their monthly wages, each taking the pool in turn. This is MUN. Weekly issue of tobacco treated similarly is called SANDE – MIPELA I MUN, and MIPELA I SANDE.

THE SOUL – It was generally believed that, in sleep, the spirit leaves the body and wanders abroad. It may have encounters with other spirits or gain knowledge on these wanderings. A dream (driman) is the consciousness of these wanderings of the spirit. A native would not awaken a sleeper abruptly, lest the spirit not have sufficient time to return to the body.
In death, the spirit permanently leaves the body and wanders in or inhabits the homeland of the deceased. In many tribes it is believed that, if the mortuary rites are properly carried out and the spirit properly propitiated, it will ward off other evil influences from the deceased's family or, at least, not be malign. It is averred that sometimes spirits are heard after a death. They indicate their presence by low whistles in the darkness. This is generally the case if a member of the deceased's family is guilty of some wrong or has broken a religious tambu.

SORCERY AND LOVE SPELLS – MALIRA, PAPAIT, and POISON (see dictionary) depend for their success on the fact that the victim is aware that they have been performed. A man or woman who is the victim of MALIRA, of PAPAIT or of sorcery, firmly believes that he, or she, is powerless against its influence. They seriously tender evidence of MALIRA or PAPAIT as a defence in cases of adultery. Legally this fails, however, as British law takes no cognizance of sorcery or magic. Belief in sorcery or magic is very strong, but it is admitted that it is generally powerless against Europeans because "EM I NARAKAIN". Failure to work is no evidence against sorcery, because it can always be explained away be presuming a fault in procedure, violation of a tambu by the sorcerer or by the presence of stronger, protective magic. See also SANGGUMA.

THE SPIRIT WORLD – The spirit world is inhabited by Dewel, Tambaran, Masalai. A *Dewel* is a deceased's spirit and may be malign or tutelary depending on whether it is shown proper respect or on whether the mortuary rites have been performed properly and no one has broken the mortuary tambus. Its abode is fixed to the area in which the death that released it occurred. *A Tambaran* is a spirit or ghost which inhabits specific areas. They may be inoffensive or they may have special functions such as bringing good crops, warding off sickness, revenging broken tambus or punishing evildoers. They must be shown proper respect and be properly propitiated if they are to perform their functions or to refrain from bringing ill-luck. They are not malign in themselves, but become so through man's negligence or misconduct. They are a great standby in native communities for keeping the women in their place. Some Tambarans have special functions at rites and ceremonies, particularly initiation ceremonies. A *Masalai* is a demon or evil spirit and inhabits some special place such as a mountain or swamp which is known as a "ples Masalai". He is essentially evil towards all men and women who enter his domain.

There is no chief spirit governing the spirit world, but in some places a spirit may be singled out as possessing greater powers, or powers relating to the more important events in native life, or as being more terrible if offended.

X

EXAMPLES OF PIDGIN-ENGLISH COMPOSITION

Translation of Anthony's Speech, Julius Caesar
Act III, Scene 2

Pren, man bilong Rom, Wantok, harim nau. Mi kam tasol long plantim Kaesar. Mi no ken beten longen. Sapos sampela wok bilong wanpela man i stret; sampela i no stret; na man i dai; ol i wailis long wok i no stret tasol. Gutpela wok bilongem i slip; i lus nating long graun wantaim long Kalopa. Pasin bilong yumi man. Maski Kaesar tu, gutpela wok i slip.

Brutus hia tokim yu long Kaesar i mangal. Sapos olsem, bikpela pekato tru. Tasol Kaesar Kalopa bekim pinis long virua bilongem. Tru, Brutus, na ol pren bilongem, gutpela man. I orait. Ol i gipim mi orait long mi toktok sori hia long Kaesar.

Kaesar hia pren bilong mi tru. Gutpela tasol long mi. Brutus kolim em mangal. Tasol Brutus gutpela man tu. Em i giaman? Olsem wonem?

Kaesar pasim planti man moa, bringim kalabus long Rom baimbai wantok baim kot bilongem na moni bilong gauman i pulap. I no save pasim moni. Olsem wonem? Pasin hia bilong Kaesar, i mangal?

Long taim ol rabisman taronggu kraikrai, Kaesar tu im I sori na krai. Mangal noken olsem; im i hat moa. Tasol Brutus kolim em mangal tumas.

Taim bilong Lupakal, yu yet lukim mi, mi laik mekim King long Kaesar. Em i rausim bek. No laik bighet. Em i sem. Tripela taim mi laik mekim; tripela taim em i rausim bek. Em i strong. Olgeta yu lukim. Im hia mangal? Tasol Brutus kolim olsem. Nau im hia gutpela man mekim dispela tok? Olsem wonem? Pasin i stret?

Aidono Brutus.

Tasol mi no laik tok nogut long Brutus. Mi no laik krosim em long giaman bilongem. Tasol mi toktok long samting ai bilong mi yet i lukim, mi save tru. Mi no ken haitim.

Long taim bipo yupela hamamas tumas long Kaesar. Em i stret. Watpo yu noken sori longem nau?

Anewe, yupela olsem wailpik. No gat save. Bel bilong yu pulap long kunai tasol!

Mi sori tumas long Kaesar kalopa slip long bokis hia. Wet liklik. Maus bilong mi heve long sori. Mi nogut nau.

THE NATIONAL ANTHEM

Deo sambai long Kwin
Sambai long Kwin bilong mi
Sambai long Kwin.

Gipim biknem long ol,
Stapgut, na winim ol,
Longtaim Kwin tasol,
Sambai long Kwin.

SOME ORIGINAL VERSE

(1) O Kanai, Kanai antap tru,
 Yu trip tasol yu go
 Mi liklik manki lukim yu,
 Mi sanap daunbilo.

 O Kanai, Kanai stap antap
 Naispela trip b'long yu
 Aitingk yu lukim Deo stap
 Na yu laik stap klostu.

(2) Liklik pisin, pren b'long mi
   Kam sindaun klostu
   Mi no meknais, nau yu kam
   Kaikai pikus tu.

   Liklik pisin, yu no pret,
   Mi no holim spia
   Naispela pisin, nau yu kam
   Liklik manki hia.

A BOY'S PRAYER TO HIS ANGEL GUARDIAN

O Anggelo bilong mi tru
Mi raring nau i go long yu
Bai yu sambai gut long mi.

Mi taronggu daunbilo
No gat strong, O Anggelo,
Satan mekim pundaun mi.

Bringim nem b'long mi i go
Long ai b'long Yesus, Anggelo
Nogut Yesus lusim mi.

Holimpas long han b'long yu
Ol raring b'long mi tu,
Gipim Yesus, King b'long mi.

Im tasol, O Anggelo,
Mi raring pinis, na mi go:
Sambai gut tumas long mi.

XI

NUMERALS

Cardinal

1	wan	10	ten
2	tu	11	wanpela ten wan
3	tri	12	wanpela ten tu
4	foa	13	wanpela ten tri
5	faiv	20	tupela ten
6	sikis	21	tupela ten wan
7	seven	30	tripela ten
8	et	31	tripela ten wan
9	nain	100	wan handet

Ordinal

1st	namba wan	3rd	namba tri
2nd	namba tu	4th	namba foa

Numeral Adjectives and Multiplicators

Once	wanpela
Twice	tupela
Thrice	tripela
Four times	foapela
Ten times	tenpela
Eleven times	wanpela ten wan
Twenty-two times	tupela ten tu

INDICATING NUMBERS WITH THE HAND

1 2 3 4 5

The two clenched fists put together indicate 10.

XII

OUTLINE OF PIDGIN ENGLISH

Introduction

Pidgin English, Tokboi, Tok Pisin or Neo-Melanesian is a native language, Melanesian in idiom and grammar. The natives of New Guinea are traditionally users of pidgin or trade languages. Long before the white man settled pidgin languages were used in the trading that seasonally took place between different language groups. A prominent example of a highly developed pidgin native language is Police Motu or Trade Motu.

Pidgin English was a natural outcome of contact with Englishmen and has far outstripped the pidgin native languages in vocabulary and distribution. As far as the T.N.G. is concerned, Pidgin English is, for all practical purposes, universal and is the recognised lingua franca. It is spoken on the mainland and adjacent islands of N.G., in the Admiralty group, New Ireland, New Britain, Solomons and has penetrated in Papua and West Irian near the T.N.G. border. While the natives speak their own language within their groups, they invariably use Pidgin English in intercourse with other language groups. Among themselves sometimes, wantoks will lapse into Pidgin English. I have indeed seen in the white settlements native children who spoke no other language but Pidgin English.

It is now, with English, the language of the House of Assembly. It is studied at the Port Moresby University and is one of the languages catered for in the Queensland University Institute of Modern Languages where it is accepted as a foreign language. Six broadcast stations use it daily; two newspapers and numerous government publications are entirely in Pidgin English, as well as the Gospels, readers, primers, text books and so on.

It must be borne in mind that Pidgin English is a *Native* language and its use is greater among natives than between native and white man. Consequently the language will remain native in idiom and syntax.

Pidgin English is a most facile language and is Melanesian. It has a vocabulary of some 1,500 words derived in the main from English and from native dialects. The best approach to it is to forget the "English" of "Pidgin English" and attack it like you would French or German. Nearly all the words derived from English have changed, limited, or extended their meanings, e.g. KILIM from "kill" means "strike a heavy blow"; SLIP from "sleep" means "lie down" or "lying"; PASIN from "fashion" means manner, procedure, action, conduct, policy, custom, habit. See the text book for BRATA and SISA which are derived from brother and sister.

You are required to have a thorough knowledge of Pidgin English for your duties in N.G. that cover police enquiries, native courts, investigations, customs complaints and civil claims, and increasingly in commerce and politics. A mastery of the language is important and a sine qua non. You must learn to think in Pidgin and understand it without having to translate. You will have to acquire the full vocabulary and be familiar with all the usages and variety of meaning of each word; metaphorical reference and implication. It will be necessary for you to be familiar with the common customs, religious beliefs, superstitions, viewpoints and institutions of the natives.

Inflection and Sound

Inflection plays an important part in what is essentially an oral language. The only way to master it properly is by observation of native speakers and then practice. You will be listening to natives from every part of New Guinea and will hear a variety of pronunciations – of consonants mostly. Many people who think they speak Pidgin English will find that natives to whom they are strangers cannot understand them. Their pronunciation is bad – more in the line of broken English. The natives round them, such as servants, have learnt to interpret what is said, but to stranger natives they are often unintelligible. Pay particular attention to pronunciation. The differences in pronunciation over the whole of N.G. are really only slight and are well known and regular.

Inflection will come naturally as you gain practice in the language. Never miss an opportunity, in your early years, to engage natives in conversation about native topics.

But the writing of the language must remain regular.

Spelling

In order to achieve good pronunciation, it is necessary to know thoroughly the orthography used to write Pidgin English. It is a system based on Dr R.A. Hall's analysis and slightly modified as described previously. All native names and words are spelt in this system. It is necessary to know it off pat, not only to learn Pidgin English from the text book, but also to enable you to accurately render names of natives, places, native words, verbatim statements, etc., and avoid confusion in village books, contracts, tax books and other documents. The occasion will arise when you will find it necessary to post notices in Pidgin English or write (or read) letters to natives.

Chapter I deals with spelling at length.

Up until the latter half of the 1950s the spelling of Pidgin English was pretty well at the mercy of those using it in publications of various sorts.

The first attempt at standardisation came in the early 1930s when the Department of District Services and Native Affairs included a direction to Field Officers in the Department's District Standing Orders to use the Royal Geographical Society's system of phonetic spelling to record personal names, place names and vocabularies.

Despite opposition to official approval of the language, Pidgin English publications increased after the war and in 1956 the Department of Education listed a Comparative Table of nine Neo-Melanesian Orthographies in use by the major publications.[1]

Clearly something had to be done. Pidgin English was the vernacular of the people and to reach them it was plain common sense to use this medium: it is now adopted as an official language of the House of Assembly, recognised as a foreign language and taught in two Universities.

Hence this book is now recast in the approved Standard Orthography.

Beliefs and Institutions

The common ones are set out in Chapter IX. If you don't know them you will miss many inferences in conversation and you will be unaware of limitations to native understanding on certain topics you wish to discuss.

It amounts to this: A word can presuppose familiarity with the workings and involved obligations to a whole system. The literal meaning of the word won't help you if you don't know its associations and inferences, e.g. SANDE, MUN, KANDERE, TAMBU.

Relationship Terms

These are based on the Melanesian Classificatory System of relationships. The biological father and his brothers are classified as PAPA, i.e. "father". The mother and her sisters are all classified as "mother" and called MAMA. To the Melanesian mind their is no need for distinction, such as in our mixed nominal and classificatory system. Therefore "papa" can sometimes be translated as "paternal uncle" and "mama" as "maternal aunt". So for a translation into English, you will have to ask if the papa mentioned is "PAPA TRU" or SMOLPAPA. This latter term is used to designate "paternal uncle" when it is necessary to differentiate, e.g. when talking to a white man. Similarly with "mama"; SMOLMAMA is "maternal aunt" for purposes of differentiation.

One of the most important relatives is the mother's brother. He is called KANDERE by his nieces and nephews and he also calls them KANDERE when addressing them. They are his KANDEREMAN and KANDEREMERI if the question of sex is important. There is a whole set of strict observances towards the mother's brother. He is an important man in the family.

1. The Standard Neo-Melanesian (Pidgin) Orthography.

BRATA and SISA are again classificatory terms and both are translateable as either brother, sister, girl cousin, boy cousin. This is their definition.

I. BRATA is a relative of the same generation and of the *Same* sex.

II. SISA is a relative of the same generation but of the *Opposite* sex.

Thus Jane's sister and girl cousin are BRATA and her brother and boy cousin are SISA. Jim's brother and boy cousin are BRATA and his sister and girl cousin are SISA.

PIKININI is the term applied to sons and daughters, nieces and nephews except your sister's children, if you are a male, who are KANDERE to you. PIKININI call their fathers and paternal uncles "PAPA" and their mothers and maternal aunts "MAMA". To differentiate, if necessary, use PIKININI MAN and PIKININI MERI. As a matter of fact, we are somewhat tautological when we say "That boy is his son". A native says "That boy is his child".

PIKININI is also the term for the young of birds and animals. PIKININI KOKORUK, PIKININI DOK – chicken and pup respectively. It is also used to name the berries and seeds of plants-

(a) Balus i Kaikai PIKININI bilong diwai.

The pigeon is eating berries of the tree.

(b) Plantim PIKININI bilong kasang.

Sow seeds of peanuts.

Grandparents are TUMBUNA; TUMBUNA MAN and TUMBUNA MERI if you want to be specific. TUMBUNA is also the term for ancestors. The term is reciprocal and grandchildren are TUMBUNA or TUMBUNA PIKININI.

Another important relative is the TAMBU. A special code of conduct is observed towards a TAMBU who is a relative by marriage such as a brother-in-law, father-in-law or sister-in-law, etc. A native never speaks the name of his TAMBU but addresses him and refers to him as "TAMBU".

Note – The word TAMBU has other meanings. It is used as a term of address to a close friend or to one whom it is desirable to placate. It is again a prohibition, something forbidden or something sacred and not to be touched. MI GAT TAMBU long PIK – I am observing a ritual abstinence from pig. LULUAI EM I TAMBUIM SINGSING – the luluai forbade the dance. EM I TAMBU – it is forbidden. TAMBU is also the name for the small currency shell – *NASSAVIUS SP.*

Clansmen are PISIN, MISMIS or BISNIS, the first being more general. These words are also the terms for clan. A member of a related clan is HAPBISNIS, or HAP PISIN –

TISPELA BOY EM I HAP PISIN BILONG MI.

This chap belongs to a clan related to mine.

(This boy he he HAP PISIN of me.)

I am inclined to think the correct term is PISIN, because birds prevail in clan totems and myth, although snakes, crocodiles, fish and pigs get a look in. BISNIS and MISMIS, I think are corruptions.

Gesture

Not much gesture is used beyond facial expression – at least no more gesture than we use in English. A typical gesture is the indicating of direction with the chin and lower lip. Sometimes a negative is indicated by a single jerk of the head to right or left and an affirmative by a jerk of the head upwards. This latter is also used sometimes when a stranger native does not understand what you are saying and is not much interested in it anyway.

See page 35 of the book for indicating numerals with the hand. This is used nearly everywhere, though I have seen a few groups that indicate by holding the fingers *Up*. For Pidgin English fingers down is the correct method.

Beckoning is done by holding the palm downwards with arm extended and jerking one's hand downwards oneself.

Negative and Affirmative

Some confusion arises at first because the native has actually a more logical approach to answering a negative question. He affirms or denies the negative in a question, e.g. KIAP I NO KAM IET? and if the kiap has not indeed come, the native replies "YES", meaning YES, *He hasn't come*. IM I NOLAIK WOK? Reply "NOGAT" (no), meaning "NO, that isn't the case" (of not wanting to work). After all, a negative question seeks an affirmative to what is stated in the question and which is believed to be the case.

Exactness in Speech

Ordinarily exactitude in terminology is often not required, e.g. LIKLIK DOKTA and DOKTA. The former means "medical assistant" (or "minor" doctor) and the latter means "doctor". Both, to the natives are doctors, and unless he wants to identify someone, he won't bother about differentiation. DOKTA I LAIK KAM GIVIM SIUT LONG YUPELA. The doctor is coming to give you injections. "Doctor" is a minor concern of the statement – the meat is "injection". Similarly with PIKININI and PIKININI MAN; PLANTI and numbers above about ten; and many others you will meet. You will find that sufficient reliability is given within the context of an account.

Many words have any one of several interpretations depending upon its *Contextual nature*, or upon the use of special modifiers with them, e.g., PASIN can mean custom, policy, conduct, action, manner, etc.; HAUS meaning shed, house, building, shelter becomes kitchen (HAUS KUK), stable (HAUS HOS), bank (HAUS MONI), office (HAUS PEPA), hospital (HAUS SIK); I GAT at the head of a phrase or sentence is "there is" and the context denotes number and tense; after a subject it means "has" or "owns" and the context again denotes number and tense. These will be dealt with later in more detail.

The Mind, Emotions and Desires

The native, away from sophistication, believes that these are seated in the belly, more intensely in the liver. This is reflected in certain forms of expression, the literal meaning of which would look strange in English. Therefore, instead of translating words, we must translate idioms. The word for belly is BEL and for liver is LIVA. When a native is endeavouring to recollect something-

> EM I ASKIM LIVA BILONGEM.
> (He, he asks liver his.)
> He is asking his liver; or in our idiom, "He is searching his memory"; i.e. trying to recollect.
> ASKIM GUT LIVA BILONG YU.
> (Ask well liver of you.)
> Examine your conscience.

If he is feeling pleased about something
> BEL BILONGEM I ORAIT LONG ...
> (Belly his it well-disposed about ...)
> He is pleased about ...
> MEKIM ORAIT BEL BILONGEM.
> (Make well-disposed belly his.)
> Put him in good humour.

Here are some examples-
> EM I MEKIM HAT BEL BILONGEM.
> (He he makes hot belly his.)
> He works himself up. (Or puts himself in a frame of mind to carry out some aggressive enterprise such as war, murder, sorcery or revenge.)
> BEL BILONG MI I HAT.
> (belly of me it hot.)
> I am angry (or roused).
> BEL BILONG MERI I TANIM NAU LONG MAN HIA.
> (belly of girl it turns now to man this.)

The girl's desires (or longings) settle now on this man (already mentioned).
MI LUSIM TRU LONG BEL BILONG MI.
(I forget truly in belly of me.)
It has gone entirely out of my mind.
LIVA BILONG MI I NO INAP LONG SAVE.
(Liver of me it not able to know.)
My mind cannot grasp (such and such).

BEL and LIVA, of course, have their ordinary meanings. BEL means commonly abdomen and belly. It is used to denote pregnancy – MERI I GAT BEL (woman she has belly), "the woman is pregnant". The fuselage of an aeroplane is called BEL – OL I PUTIM KAGO NISAIT LONG BEL BILONG BALUS (they place goods inside of belly of aeroplane), "they load the freight into the fuselage of the 'plane". LIVA is liver and WETLIVA is the term for lung.

Pitfalls

Chapter VIII deals with the spectacular faux pas. They show that a certain amount of application to the study of the language is necessary.

Numerals

Many native languages in T.N.G. have numbers only up to ten – some only five. Thereafter, in general conversation, "many" or "plenty" are used instead of the actual numbers. In Pidgin English there is a general tendency towards this too, though where counting is required it is done and accurately. Natives are not used to big numbers and only imagine them vaguely. (So do we when it gets up round the thousands.) I had a Sergeant of Native Police once – a very sophisticated native. During a talk, of which a certain pinnance was the subject, he gravely opined that its value would be about "one hundred thousand three pounds".

Among native police and sophisticated natives the ordinary English numerals are used, but otherwise the Pidgin English method is as shown on page 35.

Time

Days of the Week

SANDE   FONDE
MANDE   FRAIDE
TUNDE   SARERE
TRINDE

Months – Same as English, but spelling and pronuncation as under:

JANUERE	JULAI
FEBUERE	AUGUS
MARS	SETEMBA
APRIL	OKTOBA
MAI	NOVEMBA
JUN	DISEMBA

Very often the months are named as NAMBA WAN MUN, NAMBA TU MUN, NAMBA TRI MUN, etc.

The years are numbered as in English, e.g. 1966.

Time – The clock is used and quoted to mark the fleeting hours.

The more prominent parts of the day are as follows-

Dawn	haptulait		Midday hours	biksan
Morning	monitaim		Afternoon 4-6 p.m	apinun
Noon	belo		Night	tudak
One O'clock	belobek		Midnight hours	biknait
Five O'Clock	belo pinis			

The adjective "night" is NAIT, e.g. "WOK NAIT" – "night working".

Tomorrow	tumora
Day after tomorrow	hap tumora
2 days after tomorrow	hap tumora moa
3 days after tomorrow	hap tumora moa iet
Yesterday	asade
Day before yesterday	hap asade; asade bipo
3 days ago	tripela de bipo; tripela de i lus
For 3 days	long tripela de
Last Sunday	long sande i lus pinis; sande bipoa; long sande yumi lusim
(I've been here since Sunday)	Sande mi kam na mi stap; mi kam long sande na mi stap wet
A year later	wan yiar behain
A year longer	wan yiar moa
Until one year is up	inap long wan yiar
A year went by	wan yiar i lus

Every day	long olgeta de
Daily	oltaim long de
Occasionally	samtaim; long wanpela de, wanpela de
Often	planti taim

"Every time" or "each time" is recast into "whenever" and translated by SAPOS ... ORAIT, e.g. *SAPOS* PIKININI I KRAIKRAI, *ORAIT* MAMA I MAS GERAP – *"every time* the baby cries, its mother has to get up".

Sande – Besides meaning Sunday, it is sometimes used to mean spend Sunday, e.g. MIPELA *SANDE* LONG LAE – "We *spent Sunday* at Lae". It has another meaning too which is mentioned on page 30 of the book, i.e. the pooling of the weekly tobacco ration and one of the members taking the pool each week in turn.

Space

The white man is often confused and exasperated by such terms as LONGWE LIKLIK and KLOSTU LIKLIK and I NO LONGWE. You will be too, until you understand that a native's idea of near and far differs from ours. What is near, or a short distance away, by native standards is not by any means so according to ours. You must adapt yourself to the native standard-

KLOSTU – near. KLOSTU LIKLIK – fairly near.
LONGWE – distant. LONGWE LIKLIK – fairly distant.
KLOSTU TUMAS – very near. KLOSTU MOA – nearer.
LONGWE TUMAS – very distant. LONGWE MOA – further.
MOA LIKLIK – a little further. I NO LONGWE – not far.
LIKLIK KLOSTU – pretty near.
LIKLIK LONGWE – pretty far.

Length:

The only unit of length in Pidgin English is PRAM, "a fathom", but is measured from fingertip to fingertip of the outstretched arms. DISPELA BEKLAIN I 5 PRAM – This rope is 5 fathoms (approx.) long.

Sometimes LEK is used "to measure" in steps (1/2 pace) – HAUMAS LEK? – how many yards (steps).

Place: HAP – there. PUTIM LONG HAP – Put it there.
HAPSAIT – other side. WOKABAUT LONG HAPSAIT – Walk on the other side (of river, road, etc.).
HAPIGO – towards (away from speaker). HAPIGO LONG HAUS.
HAPIKAM – towards (towards speaker). HAPIKAM LONG MI.
LONG HAP BILONG WEWAK – in the Wewak District.

LONG HAP BILONG PAPUA – in the territory of Papua.
LONG HAP BILONG BUANG – in the Buang area.
PUTIM LONG WANPELA HAP – put it in some place.
EM I GO LONG HAP – he went in that direction.
BRINGIM LONG HAP – bring it this way.
ANTAP – above. DAUNBILO – below.
NISAIT – inside, within. ARATSAIT – outside.
ANANIT – underneath.

Contextual Nature

Contextual nature has been referred to previously. In Pidgin English, many words depend on their contextual nature for their proper meaning, i.e. on their position in, and relation to, the context, and by the use of special modifiers usually and regularly associated with such words to indicate a special particular meaning not indicated by the word standing alone. Following are common examples of such words. Some you will have already noted such as BEL, HAP, SANDE, TAMBU, etc.

AITINGK comes from "I think", but very often means "I don't know", "I suppose so", "I wonder", when it is used on its own, i.e. not in a sentence.

AITINGK mi stap tupela wik long Lae.
I think I'll stop in Lae for two weeks.
Siut i ken pen, na nogat? AITINGK.
Will the injection hurt, or not? *I don't know.* (It might and it might not.)
Em i gat planti moni laka? AITINGK
He has a lot of money, hasn't he? *I suppose so.*
Em i dai long sik, na poisin na olsem wonem? AITINGK.
Did he die from illness or sorcery or what? *I wonder.*

AS:
Ailan hia em i AS bilong balus – this island is the *breeding place* of pigeons.
Dispela dok em i AS bilong kros – this dog is the *cause* of the quarrel.
Sanap long AS bilong diwai – stand at the *stump* of the tree.
AS bilong motoka – *rear* of car.
Paitim em long AS – beat him on the *buttocks*.
AS melum melum – decrepit.
Pait nating, nogat AS bilongem – just a fight, no *reason* for it.
Mi laik paindim AS bilong dispela tok – I want to get to *the bottom* of this rumour.

BRUKIM from "broke".
> BRUKIM lap lap, putim long bokis.
> *Fold* the cloth, put it in the box.
> BRUKIM graun.
> *Dig* the ground up.
> Em i BRUKIM bun.
> He *broke* a bone.
> Yu noken BRUKIM tok bilong mipela.
> You are not to *interrupt* our conversation.

DAI comes from "die" but does not mean to die unless you use DAI PINIS, or unless DAI refers to the distant past, or to some inanimate object such as engine or fire.
> Oleman, mi DAI long kaikai taro.
> Oh dear, I *long* to eat taro.
> Dokta mekim DAI em long marasin.
> The doctor *anaesthetized* him with a drug.
> Han bilong mi i DAI.
> My hand is *numb*.
> Tumbuna i DAI longtaim bipo.
> My grandparents *died* a long time ago.
> Em i DAI PINIS
> He is *dead!*
> Mi paitim askit bilongem na em i pundaun DAI.
> I punched his jaw and he fell *unconscious*.
> Em i drink planti wiski na i DAI OLGETA.
> He drank a lot of spirit and went into a *coma* (flaked out).
> No, mi no paitim. Em i DAI long pret tasol.
> No, I didn't hit him. He just *fainted* with fright.
> MEKIM DAI masin.
> *Switch off* the engine.
> MEKIM DAI paia.
> *Extinguish* the fire.
> Tok i DAI nau!
> No more comment! ("Let the talk *cease*.")

GIAMAN: Natives generally and traditionally have quite different ideas about truth to what we have. It is not a very valuable commodity with them and its absence is not always malicious. Inaccuracies, errors and lies have about the same moral value and about the same philosophical value. In native society there is such a thing as "story prestige" or the fame and regard given to a good raconteur, because gossip and news telling is a major recreation. Truth and exactitude is subordinate to entertainment value. A thread of truth is sufficient. The natives are not alone in that. Our own press compares very favourably in that accomplishment. There is no moral sanction against lying in native communities and no opprobrium is attached to it. You therefore find that GIAMAN means "lie", "pretend", "feint", "be in error", "be incorrect", "wrong", etc. In several native dialects that I have looked into, I find the same thing.

Klok i GIAMAN - the clock is *wrong*.

No, mi GIAMAN - no, I'm *wrong*.

Em i GIAMAN long masta - he *deceived* the gentleman.

Nau, mi no GIAMAN - Now I'm not *kidding*.

Em i GIAMAN long slip - he *pretended* to be asleep.

Em i no dai, kiap i GIAMAN - he is not dead, the kiap is *mistaken*.

Mi GIAMANIM long hap abus - I *lured* (it) with a piece of meat.

Maski pasim strong, GIAMANIM tasol - don't worry about securing it, just tie it *loosely*.

HALIVIM from help: means either, assist, relieve or replace.

Kam HALIVIM mi long bokis hia.

Come and *help* me with this box.

Yu go HALIVIM wos.

Go and *relieve* the guard.

Plank i stink, HALIVIM long hap kapa.

The board is rotted, *replace* it with a piece of corrugated iron.

HAMBAK:

HAMBAK long rot - *dawdle*.

Spos yu HAMBAK, mi paitim yu - if you *play up*, i'll beat you.

Yu noken HAMBAK long meri bilong Kaiwa - you are not to *flirt* with the Kaiwa girls.

Em i HAMBAK long kaikai tasol - he is only *trifling* with his food.

Dispela hos i HAMBAK - this horse is *wayward*.

Em i no gat gutpela tingtingk em i HAMBAK tasol.

He has no nous, he's just an *aimless* fellow.

HAP: This word is dealt with in part in section SPACE, p.45. It has another meaning - portion, piece.

Man i holim HAP diwai - the man held a *bit* of wood.

Givim mi long HAP taro - give me a *piece* of taro.

KIL: Besides being a "keel" is also used to describe a sharp mountain ridge and the ridge of a house top.

LAKA: This is a word much used in Pidgin English. It is a rhetorical interrogative at the end of a statement framed as a question. The French "n'est ce pas" translates it very well. Actually it asks confirmation of the statement contained in the question. In another sense, it means "understand?"

Em i luluai, LAKA? – he's the luluai, *isn't he?*
Mi nilim kes, LAKA? – I'll nail the case, *shall I?*
Paindim gut, LAKA? – Search well, *understand?*
Kiap i laik kam, LAKA? Orait, yumi pasim pik.
The kiap is coming, *see?* So we'll catch a pig (for him).
Em i gat sik LAKA? – He is ill, *is he?*

LONGTAIM AND LONG TAIM: Mean different things. As you see one is a single word and the other is two words.
   LONG TAIM mi no kaikai – *when* I didn't eat.
   LONGTAIM mi no kaikai – *for a long time* I didn't eat.
   LONG TAIM BILONG ..... means "during".
   LONG TAIM BILONG tumbuan – *during* the Tumbuan season.
   LONG TAIM BILONG kiap Townsend – *during* Mr Townsend's *term*.

MAK, MAKIM: Mak comes from the German "mark" when its meaning is shilling. Its other meaning doubtless comes from the English "mark".
   Yu pe haumas MAK? – How many *shillings* did you pay?
   Plet i gat naispela MAK – The plate has a pretty *pattern*.
   Em i MAK bilong Bipi – it is Burns Philp's *brand*.
   Dispela hat, em i MAK bilong luluai – this hat is the *symbol* of the luluaiship.
   Bokis i nogat MAK – the box has no *brand, label, address.*
   Ol i putim MAK long diwai – they put a *sign* on the tree.
   Masta MAK – surveyor.

The transitive verb, MAKIM, is seldom used to mean "make a mark on" – better "putim mak long ..." It is, properly speaking, used to "indicate", "demonstrate" (action or speech), "choose".
   MAKIM dispela man, bai mi lukim – *point out* this man so I can look him over.
   MAKIM STRET TOK BILONGEM – *say exactly* what he said.
   Mi MAKIM em long Luluai – I *chose* him to be Luluai.
   MAKIM gut na paia – *take* good *aim* and fire.
   Kesim stik na MAKIM olgeta ples long wetsan – take a stick and *indicate* (the position of) on the sand all the villages.

NATING: Comes from "nothing". It is frequently used in colloquial English in the T.N.G. Chapter VII covers it sufficiently.

PAINIM: Comes from "find", but very often means "look for", "meet".
   PAINIM gut laka? – *search* well, understand?
   Mi PAINIM gut tumas, tasol mi no lukim – I *searched* thoroughly, but I couldn't find it.
   Go PAINIM long haus – go and *look* (for it) in the house.

Mi PAINIM, tasol i bagarap – I *found* it but it is ruined.
Mi wokabaut long rot na PAINIM wanpela meri – I walked along the road and *met* a girl.
Tultul i PAINIM naip long rot, na gipim long Kiap – the tultul *found* the knife on the road and gave it to the Kiap.

You will notice that another part of the sentence indicates that the article is found.

PASIM from "fasten".
PASIM kanu long bris.
Tie the canoe to the jetty.
PASIM dua.
Shut the door.
Mi laik go, tasol kiap PASAIM mi.
I wanted to go, but the kiap *detained* me.
Diwai PASIM rot.
A tree *blocks* the road.
PASIM lain!
Hold the carriers.
PASIM tok.
Stop talking.
Orait, PASIM tultul.
Righto, *arrest* the tultul.
PASIM ol long banis.
Secure them in the enclosure.

PASIN from "fashion". It covers a wide field of meanings, all somewhat synonymous, e.g. conduct, behaviour, policy, procedure, line of action, manner, way, custom, habit, practice, etc.

Yu noken sakim tok bilong papa. Em i PASIN nogut.
You mustn't disobey your father. That's bad *conduct*.

PASIN bilong dispela masin i olsem.
The *action* of this engine is like this.
Kuskus i nosave long PASIN bilong kot.
The clerk doesn't understand court *procedure*.
Waria i nogat PASIN olsem.
The Waria people haven't such a *custom*.
PASIN bilong Masta Jones i olsem.
Such is Mr Jones' *habit*.
Em i mekim long wonem PASIN?
In what *manner* did he do it?
PASIN bilong meri tasol.
Just the *way* of women.

PASIN bilong Gavman i bilong halivim yupela.
The *policy* of the Government is to assist you.
Yu noken kros long ai bilong Kiap. Em i PASIN nogut.
You mustn't quarrel in front of the Kiap. That's bad *manners*.
Kot i no stret. I mekim PASIN NOGUT long mi.
The court is unfair. It did an *injustice* to me.
Em i man bilong poison. Em i save mekim PASIN NOGUT TRU.
He is a sorcerer. He can do *very wicked things*.

PREN comes from "friend". Means "friend", but also means "lover" and is used, in addition, as a friendly term of address.

Dispela man em i PREN bilong mi.
This man is my *friend*.
Dispela meri i gat PREN long boskru.
This girl has a *lover* in the crew.
No PREN, mi noken stilim moni bilong yu.
No *friend*, I wouldn't steal your money.
Meri i PREN longem tasol. Tupela i no marit.
The girl only *gave herself* (as a lover) to him. They are not married.

SAMTING comes from "something". SAMTING is a very useful word meaning an "article" a "thing" or a *personal matter*.

SAMTING bilong yu – your *business* or *affair*
SAMTING bilong pasim lok – a *thing* to secure a lock (key).
SAMTING nogut – evil or bad *thing*.
SAMTING natink – *thing* of no consequence.
SAMTING tru – *thing* of consequence or value; the real thing.
Pasim laplap: nogut ol i lukim SAMTING bilong yu.
Tie your lavalava lest people see your *privates*.
(In this connection, SAMTING is the polite term for the male genitals.)
Wonem SAMTING? – what do you want? What's the matter?
Em SAMTING bilong wonem? – What's that (*thing*) for?
Kesim OLGETA SAMTING – get *everything*.
Sipos yu gat SAMTING i bruk – if you have *anything* that's broken.

SAVE probably comes from French "savez" or Spanish "sabe" via Cantonese Pidgin English.

Yu SAVE Master Smith? – do you *know* Mr Smith?
Mi SAVE tokboi – I *understand* Pidgin English.
Mi SAVE masin – I *know how to operate* the engine.
Mi no SAVE les – I am not *accustomed* to loaf.
Mi SAVE siut – I *can* shoot.
Noken hambak, SAVE? – No playing up, *understand?*
Mi no SAVE – I don't *know*.

Em i nogat SAVE – he has no *brains*.

PIPIA, RABIS, RABISMAN: PIPIA is the word for "rubbish" and though RABIS is derived from "rubbish" it does not mean "rubbish". It means "poor", "poverty stricken".

    Brumim PIPIA – sweep up the *rubbish*.

    A, PIPIA tasol, tromwe – Ah nothing but *rubbish*, pitch it out.

    Ples i RABIS – the village is *poverty stricken*.

    Mi no moa got moni, mi RABIS tasol – I no longer have any money, I am *penniless*.

    Em i RABISMAN – he is a *poor man* (beggar).

A RABISMAN is a person without possessions and they are occasionally present in native communities. They are despised.

PAUDA from "powder", but means "firecrackers", or occasionally "gunpowder". It does not mean "talcum powder", which is translated by KAMPANG SMEL.

SEM comes from "shame" but its meaning really is "embarrassment" or "shyness".

    Sanap klostu, yu no ken SEM – stand near, don't be *shy*.

    Kiap i lap na mi SEM – the kiap laughed and I was *embarrassed*.

    No gat SEM bilong yu? – aren't you *ashamed* of yourself?

Metathesis

Many words derived from English have undergone change in meaning, pronunciation and spelling. Their etymons very often offer no clue to their Pidgin meaning and consequently many white men misinterpret them. The more prominent of them are listed below. Some have already occurred in section 14 and we won't repeat them here.

BAIM, PEIM, SALIM from "buy", "pay" and "send". BAIM means "to buy" but also means "to pay".

    Mi BAIM kokoruk – I *buy* a fowl.

    Mi BAIM tultul long 5 mak – I *paid* the tultul 5/-.

    Mi BAUM tultul long trabel bilong mi – I *recompensed* the tultul for my offence.

    Mi BAIM kot – I *pay* fine.

PEIM only means to "sell", though PE is "payment" or "wages".

    Mi PEIM banana long kiap – I *sold* bananas to the kiap.

    Givim PE long ol wokboi – give the labourers their *wages*.

    Mi laik kesim PE long pik – I wish to receive *payment* for the pig.

    Yu noken PEIM long liklik PE – you mustn't *sell* it for a small *payment*.

The origin of SALIM seems to be confused between "sell" or to "give", even though sometimes, under the Law of Reciprocation, payment or a return gift is expected.

    Mi SALIM meri long wok – I *sent* the woman to the garden.
    MI SALIM kaukau long tultul – I *gave* some kaukau to the tultul.
    SALIM pas long kiap – *send* a note to the kiap.

GRAS from "grass". It very seldom is used to mean grass but is one of the common words you will pick up quite early. It means "hair", "fur", "feathers".

    GRAS bilong muruk – Cassowary *feather*.
    GRAS bilong kapul – Possum's *fur*.
    Katim GRAS bilong mi – Cut my *hair*.
    Maus GRAS – Beard (Mouth *hair*).
    GRAS bilong sipsip – wool (Sheep's *hair*).
    No kunai, i narakain GRAS – It's not kunai, it's a different *grass*.

KILIM from "kill" but never means "kill" except by inference.

KILIM I DAI is "kill".

    Diwai i KILIM em – a tree *fell on* him.
    Em i KILIM meri long hap diwai – he *struck* the woman with a billet of wood.
    Sotwin KILIM mi – yearning *affects* me *deeply*.
    Oleman, soa i KILIM mi tru – 'struth, the ulcer is really *hurting* me.
    KILIM i dai – *kill* it.
    KILIM pik long tomiok – *kill* the pig with an axe.
    In this latter it is obvious that to strike a pig with a lethal weapon is meant to kill it.

KOL comes from "cold" but also means "damp" as an adjective and "dew" as a noun; also "shade".

    Mi KOL tumas – I am very *cold*.
    KOL i kamdaun long nait – *dew* fell at night.
    Laplap i KOL – the lavalava is *damp*.
    Sindaun long ples KOL – sit in the *shade*.

LUS, LUSIM; from "lose" and "loose". LUS is a passive intransitive verb or might even be considered as an adjective. Its meaning is "dead" or "lost" in the sense that one's life is lost.

    Em i LUS long solwara – he was *drowned* in the sea.
    Em i LUS long pait – he was *killed* in battle.
    Moni bilong mi i LUS – my money is *gone* (lost).
    Mi no save, aiting i LUS – I don't know, I think it was *lost*.

LUSIM is the transitive verb but its meaning changes to "forget", "leave behind", "loosen". It does not now mean "lose".

Mi LUSIM nem bilong tultul – I *forget* the tultul's name.
Mi LUSIM James long wara – I *left* James *behind* at the river.
Mi LUSIM tabak long haus – I *left* my tobacco in the house.
Mi no ken LUSIM yupela – I won't *forget* you all.

MEKIM comes from "make", and when it is used as an auxiliary verb, it means "to make"; otherwise it means "to do" and one other meaning, "shake" or "rattle".

MEKIM dai paia – *make* to die the fire.
MEKIM nogut mi – *makes* me to be injured.
Em i MEKIM gutpela – he *did* (it) well.
MEKIM belo – *make* it ring (the bell).
Goan, MEKIM – go on, *shake* it.
Tupela i slip, na em i MEKIM – the two of them laid down and they *did* it (you know what).

MEKIM repeated several times is used to relate perseverance at some task or pursuit and is then literally "did it, did it, did it", or "worked, worked, worked", e.g. orait mipela go pianim long bus. Mekim, mekim, mekim, tasol nogat, ol i ronwe pinis – so we searched in the bush. *Searched, searched and searched.* But no result; they had all run away.

The transitive verb "make" is translated by WOKIM, e.g. Mi laik WOKIM kanu – I wish to *make* a canoe. It comes from "work". WOKIM also means "to repair", e.g. siot i bruk. Kesim nil na WOKIM – the shirt is torn. Take a needle and *repair* it.

WOKIM paia – *make* the fire.
WOKIM haus – *build* a house.
WOKIM bret – *make* some bread.
WOKIM poisin – *make* sorcery.

WOK, the noun, means besides "work", "labour", "employment", "duty" means also "garden".

Em i WOK bilong Gauman – it is a Government *job*.
Em i WOK bilong luluai – it is the luluai's *duty*.
Wonem WOK bilong yu? – what is your *employment*.
Mi go long WOK kesim taro – I'll go to the *garden* and get some taro.

As an intransitive verb, it means "work".

Mi WOK long Bipi – I *work* at Burns Philp.
WOK bus, WOK nait – bushwork, nightwork.

Translation

In translating either Pidgin into English or English into Pidgin, do it paragraph by paragraph and not word by word or even sentence by sentence. Read the paragraph through until you have the exact sense and meaning and then recast it into the idiom of the translating language. Many English clauses or phrases are parenthetical, and the sequence of ideas is not the same as in Pidgin English. The difference can perhaps be illustrated by the following pattern.

English: A, therefore C, if B.
Pidgin: A and B, therefore C.

There are a number of Pidgin English words used in colloquial English that are seldom translated, viz: KIAP, POLISMASTA, HAUS TAMBARAN, POLISBOI, LULUAI, TULTUL, BOSBOI, DOKTA BOI, GALIP, TARO, PUKPUK, PAS, KAPIAK, KAIKAI, SAKSAK, etc,; also some words cannot be translated direct, e.g. OWNER. A transposition must be made like this: "*I am the owner* of this pig" transposed to "This pig *bilongs to me.*"

Mistranslations

Below are a number of words very frequently mistranslated-

AIDONO is "I don't know so-and-so's feelings, intentions, etc." not "I don't know". It is a transitive verb.
BEKSAIT is "back" or "rear" not "buttocks".
DEVEL means "shadow", "soul" and not "devil".
KAM WAU is come *from* Wau. Kam *LONG* Wau is come *to* Wau.
KLOSAP means "nearly", e.g. KLOSAP mi pundaun – I nearly fell down.
KLOSTU means *"near"*, e.g. Haus i KLOSTU – the house is near.
LUKAUTIM means "take care of" and not "look for".
MAUS BILONG WARA is a barbarism and does not translate "river mouth" which is LEK BILONG WARA. The source is AI BILONG WARA.
MEME is pith or dregs or fibre left out of something eaten and is not "goat" which is ME.
MIPELA is always plural and does not include the person spoken to. YUMI includes the person spoken to and is plural or dual.
NAU WONEM is rhetoric, meaning "of course", "naturally", "what else?" It does not mean "what's up now?", "what do you want?"
PES means "forehead" and not "face".
PULIM almost always means "persuade", "inveigle", "obliged"; less

often "rape", "force".

PUSHIM means "copulate with" and not "push". SIUBIM is the word for "push".

STAP means "be present", "remaining", etc., and not "finish" or "ended".

SI is a "stormy sea" or "waves" not "sea". Sea is SOLWARA.

Writing

In written Pidgin English natives show a variety of interpretation of the phonetics of the language. This is due to the fact that Pidgin English was until latterly an oral language. Again New Guinea languages have different phonetic milieux that colour each speaker's pronunciation. The oft-quoted example, of course, is L and R – some natives pronouncing R as L, and others, L as R. However, the best course for you is to follow the system in the text book. After some practice in reading, you will recognise the variations without hesitation. Chapter I deals with them, but the main things is a standard orthography.

In writing Pidgin English words, or native words as quotes in an English text, or documents, always write them in *printed capitals*.

CLASSIFIED VOCABULARY

For fuller detail, see general vocabulary.

The Body

AI – eye
AI RAUN – dazed
AI PAS – blind
AS – buttocks
ASKIT – jaw
AS MELUM MELUM – very old
BANIS – ribs
BEKSAIT – back
BEL – abdomen; mind
BLUT – blood
BOKIS – vagina
BOL – scrotum
BONAN – muscles behind the kidneys and, in the wild pig, a delicious pair of fillets.
BROS – chest
BUK – boil; carbuncle
BUN – bone
DAI – unconscious; coma
DOTI – personal leavings; excreta, parings, etc.
FINGGA – finger; toe
FUT – foot
GRAS – hair
GRAS BILONG MAUS – whiskers
GRILE – tinea
GRIS – fat
HAN – arm
HAN SIUT – right hand
HANGGRE – weak; starved
HET – head
HET I PEN – headache
IA – ear
KAIS – left hand
KAN – female external genitals
KAPA – finger-, toe-nail
KAPOPO – fart
KASKAS – scabrous skin
KELA – bald
KEMPE – leprosy

KIAU – testicle
KIDNI – kidney
KOK – penis
KRU – brain
KUS – cough
LAPUN – old
LEK – leg; foot
LIVA – liver; mind
MATAKIAU – only one eye
MAUS – mouth
MELEK – semen
MIT – flesh
NEK – neck; throat
NEK I PAS – dumb
NUS – nose
PAIP – trachea
PAM – heart
PEKPEK – faeces
PEKPEK BLUT – diarrhoea; dysentery
PEN – painful; sore
PES – forehead
PISPIS – urine
PIVA – fever
POSAI – albino
PUINGA – fart
PUKPUK – in addition to meaning "crocodile", also describes a person with tinea all over his body – either *T. imbricata or t. annulata.*
RAITHAN – right hand
ROP – blood vessel; sinew
SANGANA – inside of thigh
SIK – illness
SKIN – skin
SKRU – elbows; knee
SKRU I LUS – lame
SOA – ulcer; sore
SOL – shoulder
SPET – spittle
STRONGPELA SOA – ulcer
SUSU – breasts; milk
TAMATA – nodular leprosy
TAMBILUA – yaws
TANG – tongue
TIS – tooth

TIS I PEN – toothache
TONO – corn on sole of foot, plantar wart
TRAUT – vomit
TUHAT – perspiration
WARA BILONG AI – tears
WETLIVA – lung
YAU – ear
YAU PAS – deaf

People

(For relationship terms see page 39)

AISMALANG – sodomist
ANSINI – mechanic; engineer
BAIMBOI – recruiter
BIKBEL – a fat man
BIKYADS – Judge
BIPI – Burns Philp & Co
BISOP – Bishop
BOI – native man; servant. (This word is pretty dead now though still in limited use.)
BOSBOI – native foreman
BOSKRU – crew
BRUDER – lay brother
BUSKANAKA – savage
DIDIMAN – Agric. Dept.; field-officer of same
DOKTA – medical officer
DOKTABOI – native medical orderly
DRAIVA – native driver
FAKIMHAS – one who commits sodomy on another
GAVMAN – Government
GOLMESA – Sergeant-Major
HAPKAS – half caste
INGLIS – British
KAGOBOI – carrier
KALABUS – convict, prisoner
KALOPA – one to be pitied
KAMNDA – carpenter; K- W.R. Carpenter & Company
KAMPANI – Commercial firm; any person not working for Government or mission
KANAKA – free native
KASTANS – customs

KEPTEN – captain, pilot (bilong balus)
KIAP – D.O.; A.D.O.; P.O.
KIAP BILONG BALUS – Inspector Civil Aviation
KING – King
KONGKONG – Chinaman
KOPIRUL – Corporal
KRANI – Malay
KRUTMAN – police recruit
KUK – cook; sometimes wife
KUKBOI – native cook
KUKURAI – head man
KUNDAR – altar boy
KUSKUS – clerk
LANIS KOPIRUL – L/Corporal
LAPUN – old person
LESMAN – loafer
LIKLIK DOKTA – medical assistant
LULUAI – head man
MANAMBUS – savage, primitive
MANKI – boy; youth
MANKIMASTA – personal servant
MANMERI – everybody
MANUWA – (slang) a very fat person
MASTA – Mister; M- white man; employer
MASTA KOT – lawyer
MASTA MAK – surveyor
MERI – native woman; female; wife
MERI PAMUK – harlot
MISIN – missioner; mission
MISINBOI – native catechist, teacher
MISIS – Mrs; white women; wife
MUMUT BOI – worker on sanitary squad
NAMBA WAN GAVMAN – Administrator
NAMBA WAN KIAP – District Commissioner
NAINSI – effeminate man
NASAU – dunderhead
PATER – priest
PIKININI – child
POISIN – sorcerer
POLISBOI – native constable
POLISMASTA – European Police officer
POPI – Catholic
POSAI – albino

PRANIS – Italian; Frenchman
PREN – friend; lover
PROMAN – partner, one of a pair
PULMAN – fool
RABISMAN – impoverished person, beggar, slave, no-hoper
SAINAMAN – Chinese
SAKMAN – strict, severe or stern person in authority
SAITAN – Sergeant
SANGSANGANA – twins
SAVITOK – interpreter
SELA – sailor
SEVENDE – 7th-day Adventist
SIAMAN – German
SIAPAN – Japanese
SISTA – trained nurse, nun
SIUTBOI – game-boy
SIUTMAN – policeman (old fashioned)
SKULBOI – schoolboy
SOLDIA – soldier
SUMATIN – scholar (old fashioned)
TALATALA – Protestant
TARONGGU – unfortunate person
TEMATAN – heathen (old fashioned)
TISA – teacher
TISABOI – native teacher
TULTUL – village official, interpreter and assistant to the luluai
WAITHET – paramount luluai
WOKBOI – native labourer
WOS – sentinel

Birds

BALUS – pigeon
GURIA – gaura pigeon
KANAI – gull
KLANGAL – large brilliant parrot
KOKI – cockatoo
KOKOMO – hornbill
KOKORUK – poultry
KOTKOT – crow
KUMUL – n., Bird of Paradise
LONGPELA NEK – crane, heron
MANANGUNAI – sea eagle

MARIP - small green and red parrot
MURUK - cassowary
PATO - duck
PATOGUS - goose
PAUL BILONG BUS - scrub turkey, wild fowl
PIPI - turkey
PISIN - bird
TARANGGAU - hawk, eagle
WAIL PAUL - wild fowl

Animals

BLAK BOKIS - flying fox
BONON - dugong
BULMAKAU - cattle
DOK - dog
DOKOROK - frog
DONKI - mule
HOS - horse
KAPUL - possum, cuscus
KARABU - water buffalo
LIKLIK RAT - mouse
MANG - small ratlike creature with long thin tail
ME - goat
MORAN - python, carpet snake
MUMUT - bandicoot
PALAI - lizard, iguana
PIG - pig
PUKPUK - crocodile
PUSI - cat, rabbit
RAT - rat
SIKAU - wallaby, bandicoot, kangaroo. S. bilong diwai - tree kangaroo
SIPSIP - sheep
SNEK - snake

Insects

ANIS - ant
BEMBE - butterfly
BINATANG - insect
KARAKUM - red ant
LANG - fly

LAUS – flea
MASKITA – mosquito
NATNAT – sandfly, midge
NGOSNGOS – louse
NINIK – bee
SNEK – grub, larva, worm

Fish

AINA (AINANGA) – whitebait
AMBUSA – porpoise
ATUN – tuna
BIKBEL – toadfish
BIKMAUS – cod
BLUPELAPIS – blue parrot fish
BOKIS – toadfish
DANGIL – mackerel
DOKTA – small striped fish
EPA – stingray
GAM – bailer shell
GAMSEL – clam
KARUA – mullet
KATU – hermit crab
KINA – oyster
KINDAM – prawn, crayfish, lobster
KINYA – pearl shell
KORVO – sunfish, stingray
KUKA – crab
LALA – species of shoal fish
LALAI – trochus
LANGUL – trevally
LONGPELA MAUS – gar, long tom
MAKAU – brown fish about 35.5 cms
MALAMBUL – herring
MALIO – eel
MALISA – sea pike, barracuda
MORSO – species of reef fish
PIS – fish
PISLAMA – trepang
POPIS – porpoise
SAK – shark
SAK ANGGAU – dogfish
SOPIS – swordfish

STINGRE - stingray
SUSU - white narrow fish of trevally family
TALAI - sardines
TALIBUNG - green sea snail
TAMBU - small shell used as currency
TAUKA - cuttlefish, squid
TAUL - conch shell
TORASEL - turtle
TUNA - sea eel
ULA - species of fish
URITA - octopus, squid
WUSTA - oyster

Trees, Plants, Fruits, Vegetables

(See dictionary for full description)

AIBIKA - edible leaf
AILA - large tree
ANANAS - pineapple
ANIAN - onion, shallot
ARANG - pandanus
AUPA - native spinach
BAIBAI - small stunted palm
BANANA - banana
BATA - avocado pear
BILINAT - betel-nut
BIN - bean
BLUT - sap
BOMBOM - palm frond
BRUS - leaf tobacco, tobacco plant
DAKA - pepper vine and fruit
DIWAI - any tree; wood
DRAI - ripe coconut
ERIMA - large semi-hardwood tree
FIKAS - fig tree
GALIP - south seas almond
GOLGOL - aromatic plant of ginger family
HASBIN - wing bean
HEBSEN - peas
HUM - fleshy long leafed pandanus
IROTU - callophyllum tree
KABIS - cabbage
KALAPILIM - callophyllum tree

KAMANGORO - large tree with edible tips. Also TULIP
KANGKO - watercress
KAPIAK - breadfruit
KARAPAI - wild corn
KARAPUA - short fat cooking banana
KARUKA - pandanus species
KASANG - peanut
KASTA - small nut-bearing tree; nut of same which is ground and used as gum
KAUKAU - sweet potatoes
KAUL - a small species of bamboo
KAWAWAR - ginger
KAWIWI - wild betel nut
KEPOK - kapok tree
KOKONAS - coconut and C. palm
KOLSIS - small leafed mangrove
KOPRA - dried meat of the coconut
KRAKON - bush rope vine
KUKAMBA - cucumber
KULAU - unripe coconut
KUMU - edible greens of all kinds
KUMURERE - large eucalypt
KUNAI - lalang grass
KWILA - well-known hardwood tree
LAULAU - red pear-shaped fruit, also tree bearing same. Edible, somewhat like apple - Malay Apple
LAUP - N.G. walnut
LIMBOM - hardwood palm tree
LIP - foliage, leaf
LOMBO - chilli, capsicum
MAKAS - small tree with hibiscus-like flower
MALO - species of fig tree
MAMBU - bamboo
MAMI - tuber root vegetable
MANGGROS - mangrove
MARAMAL - jacaranda
MARITA - pandanus with long red edible fruit
MAROTA - nipa palm
MELEN - melon
MULI - lime, lemon
NANAS - pineapple
NOK - flower cluster of coconut
OKARI - a very large Papuan tree with a large egg-shaped nut tasting

    like the N.G. galip
PAINAP – pineapple
PALPAL – medium sparse-leaved tree
PAMKEN – pumpkin
PAPAI – mushroom
PIT – variety of wild sugar, edible flower cluster
PITPIT – wild sugar non-edible
PLAUA – flower (also Pulpul)
POPO – pawpaw
PRUT – fruit; tinned fruit
PULPUL – flower, shrubs
PUNPUN – tree of acacia family
SAIOR – edible greens of all kinds
SAKSAK – sago palm; native sago
SAMPEPA – large shrubs with large leaves which are used by natives as sandpaper
SANG – hard straight-grained tree
SARAT – stinging nettle
SAUA – soursop
SKINDIWAI – bark
SOTPELA SWIT MULI – mandarin
SUKA – sugar cane
SWITMULI – orange
TABAK – stick tobacco
TALASA – tall tree, horizontal branches with thin-walled green nut
TALINGA – mushroom, edible fungus
TALIS – tree with edible nut; elastic durable timber
TAMBUN – medium-sized tree
TANGKET – plant to over 3 metres high; yellow, green or purple leaves which are long, shiny and oblate in spiral arrangement quite prominent in native culture
TAPIOK – cassava plant
TARO – taro, edible tuber of calla lily family
TAUN – large hardwood tree, pink to brown wood
TON – large hardwood tree
TULIP – see Kamangoro
TUMATO – Tomato
UTUN – large coastal flowering tree
YAM – yam
YAMBO – guava
YAR – casuarine

Tools

AIN – plane blade, pressing iron
AKIS – axe
BAIRA – hoe
BASKET – basket
BATARI – battery, torch cell
BEK – bag
BILO – half coconut shell used as a cup, dipper, ladle or bailer
BOA – drill, auger, brace and bit
BOKIS – box, trunk, chest
BRUM – broom
DAINAMAIT – dynamite; gelignite; also PATRON
DIWAI – wood
FAIL – file; rasp
GABEL – garden fork
GUMI – rubber
HAMA – hammer
HOBEL – plane
KALABUS – net sling
KAPA – galvanised iron
KAPA RESA – razor blade
KES – wooden box or case
KIAP – percussion cap
KIT – putty
KOLTA – tar, creosote
KOROBA – crow bar
KUKA – pincers
LATA – steps, ladder
LET – belt
LOK – lock, padlock
MAISEL – chisel: KOL SISEL – cold chisel
NAIP – knife. NAIP skru – penknife
NIL – nail, needle, pin
PAIP – piping
PAMLIL – cobbler's palm
PATRON – dynamite
PAUDA – gunpowder
PEN – paint, ochre
PIK – pick; pickaxe, mattock
PIUS – fuse
PLAIAS – pliers
PLANGK – board; plank

POLIS – metal polish
POS – post
RESA – razor
ROP – rope, cord
SAMPEPA – sandpaper
SANGGE – pincers
SAPA – adze
SARIP – grass knife
SAVEL – shovel
SEN – chain
SIMEN – cement
SISIS – scissors
SLING – sling
SO – saw
SPANA – spanner
SPED – spade
SPIRIS – methylated spirits
TAMIOK – axe, tomahawk
TAPEL – a slate
TIRAP – pedal
TRET – thread
TWAIN – string
UMBEN – fish or pig net
WAIA – wire
WEL – oil
WILKA – wheelbarrow

Household Phrases

1. Haumas klok?
   What is the time?
2. Lainim tebal.
   Set the table.
3. Bringim kaikai i kam.
   Bring the food in.
4. Mi no laik kaikai. Mi dringk ti tasol.
   I don't want to eat. I will only have a drink of tea.
5. Kapsaitim lip ti long tin.
   Tip the tea into the tin (container).
6. Opim tin talai.
   Open a tin of sardines.
7. Fasim taunam.
   Tighten the mosquito net.

8. Wokim ti.
   Make tea.
9. Laitim lam (paia).
   Light the lamp (fire).
10. Mekim dai lam.
    Put out the light.
11. Kesim pipia klos na wasim.
    Take the soiled clothing and wash it.
12. Putim waswas bilong mi.
    Prepare my bath.
13. Wok bilong yu i no stret.
    Your work is careless.
14. Bringim klinpela siot.
    Fetch me a clean shirt.
15. Moni bilong mi i stap long bak trausis.
    My money is in the trouser's pocket.
16. Kesim kiwi na klinim su.
    Get the boot polish and clean the shoes.
17. Westap let bilong me?
    Where is my belt?
18. Banisim me na pulim susu.
    Corral the goats and milk them.
19. Kukim pato long mumu.
    Cook the duck in a mumu (mumu *q.v.*)
20. Mi no laik kaikai tin mit. Kukim kiau.
    I don't wish to eat tinned meat. Cook eggs.
21. Brukim kiau i go long plet na paitim.
    Break the eggs into a bowl and beat them.
22. Paitim potete na abusim liklik sol longen.
    Mash the potatoes and mix a little salt with them.
23. Hatwara i hat iet?
    Is the water hot yet?
24. Maski kukim abus, mi kaikai kol kaikai.
    Don't bother to cook a meal, I'll eat a cold meal.
25. Gerap long tulait, wokim bret.
    Rise at dawn and make some bread.
26. Kapsaitim susu long ti.
    Pour milk into the tea.
27. Bokis kaikai i gat anis.
    There are ants in the food safe.
28. Tromwe kaikai long kokoruk.
    Throw the food to the fowls.
29. Skelim liklik rais long man hia.

      Dish out a little rice to this bloke.
30.   Tede masta Mik i kam kaikai long apinum.
      Today Mr Mick comes for the evening meal.
31.   Haumas masta bai i kam?
      How many gentlemen are coming?
32.   Go gerapim kuk.
      Go and wake the cook.

NEO-MELANESIAN TO ENGLISH

LIST OF ABBREVIATIONS

a., adjective
adv., adverb
aux., auxiliary
card., cardinal
colloq., colloquial
conj., conjunction
dem., demonstrative
excl., exclamation
fig., figurative
imp., imperative
indef., indefinite
lit., literally

miss., mission
n., noun
naut., nautical
neg., negative
num., numeral
ord., ordinal
prep., preposition
pron., pronoun
prop., proper
v., verb
v.i., verb intransitive
v.t., verb transitive

A: often pronounced as HA –.

ABRIS: *v.i.*, dodge, avoid, evade, duck; go round, circumvent.
    v.t.- ABRISIM.

ABUS: *n.*, meat, flesh; diet, food, "Daily bread".

ABUSIM: *v.t.*, mix, stir together. Also TANIM WANTAIM.

AI: *n.*, eye; lid or stopper of jar, saucepan, bottle, etc.; the very summit or top.

AI I PAS: *a.*, blind; afflicted with blight.

AI I RAUN: *a.*, be dazed, in the act of falling into a faint.

AIADIN: *n.*, iodine. Also YOT.

AIBIKA: *n.*, edible leaf of a small tripartite leafed shrub with red stem: also the shrub itself. It is cultivated by the natives. Probably *Abelmoschus Manihot*.

AIDONO: *v.*, I don't know-----'s mind, feelings, etc.

AIGLAS: *n.*, spectacles.

AILA: *n.*, large, gnarled, softwood tree with oblate leaves.

AILAN: *n.*, island, small isolated patch of bush in grassy country.

AIN: *n.*, iron or steel plane blade; an iron (laundry).

AINANGA: *n.*, whitebait. Also AINA.

AINIM: *v.t.*, iron.

AISMALANG: *n.*, sodomy, one who permits sodomy on himself.

AITINGK: *v.i.*, I think so, I reckon; I couldn't say. See p.46.

AKANGGELO: *n.*, archangel.

AKIS: *n.*, axe.

AMAT: *a.*, raw. Also NO DAN.

AMBILOK: *n.*, envelope; also SKIN-PAS, q.v.

AMBRELA: *n.*, umbrella.
AMBUSA: *n.*, porpoise.
AMI: *n.*, Army.
ANANAS: *n.*, (also NANIS, q.v.), pineapple.
ANANIT: *adv.*, under, beneath, inferior in status, below.
ANEWE: *adv.*, as a matter of fact, at any rate.
ANGGASIP: *n.*, handkerchief.
ANGGELO: *n.*, angel.
ANGGAU: *n.*, SAK ANGGAU = dogfish.
ANIAN: *n.*, onion, eschalotte.
ANIS: *n.*, ant.
ANKA: *n.*, anchor.
ANKARIM: *v.t.*, anchor.
ANTAP: *adv.*, above, over, on top; *n.*, Heaven.
ANTEK: *n.*, deck.
APIM: *v.t.*, raise.
APOSTEL: *n.*, apostle.
ARAPELA: *a.*, other.
ARASAIT: *adv.*, outside, out.
ARERE: *n.*, edge, border, boundary, limit.
AROVA: *v.i.*, change course so as to avoid obstacle (boats and vehicles).
AROVARIM: *v.t.*, steer round, sheer off.
AS: *n.*, buttocks, bottom, stump, underlying cause, place of origin, under side, rear. See p.46.
ASADE: *adv.*, yesterday.
ASADE BIPO: *adv.*, day before yesterday.
ASAWE: like that! that's the way to do it!
ASIS: *n.*, hatches.
ASIT: that's it! exactly!
ASKIM: *v.t.*, ask, make enquiries.
ASKIT: *n.*, jaw, chin.
AS MELUM MELUM: *n.*, aged person.
ASPRIN: *n.*, aspro, aspirin.
ATUN: *n.*, tunny fish.
AUPA: *n.*, native spinach (*Aramanthus gangeticus*).
AVEN: *n.*, oven.

BAGARAP: *v.i.*, break, become impaired, have an accident happen to, become exhausted or injured, disintegrate.
BAI: *conj.*, then, after that, in order that, in consequence, so that; *aux.v.*, shall, will.
BAIBAI: *n.*, short stunted palm-like tree with a feathery leaf about 1 metre long, growing from the crown of a scarred trunk, on

which is borne a single round collective fruit about 15.2 cms in diameter. The trunk may be branched and the tree lives to a great age.

BAIBEL: *n.*, Bible (also BUK-TAMBU).
BAIM: *v.t.*, buy, pay, recompense.
BAIMBAI: *adv.*, afterwards, later, in time, then (future).
BAIRA: *n.*, hoe.
BAK: *n.*, pocket. BAK TRAUSIS: *n.*, trousers' pocket.
BAKSTUA: *n.*, warehouse, bulkstore.
BAL: *n.*, ball.
BALUS: *n.*, pigeon, aeroplane.
BANANA: *n.*, banana.
BANIS: *n.*, fence, enclosure or compound; ribs; bandage.
BANISIM: *v.t.*, fence, encircle, enclose, bar.
BAPTISIMO: *n.*, baptism. Also WAS-WAS.
BARAT: *n.*, valley, drain, water race, gully, canal.
BASKET: *n.*, basket.
BASTAT: *n.*, bastard, a term of abuse.
BATA: *n.*, avocado pear – *Persea* species (also called Alligator Pear); butter, margarine.
BATEN: *n.*, button.
BATERI: *n.*, battery, torch cell. HOTIM BATERI – charge a battery.
BAUT (Naut.): *v.i.*, put about; to bow.
BAUTIM (Naut.): *v.t.*, put about.
BEK: *adv.*, back. *n.*, bag, sack.
BEKBOT (Naut.): *n.*, port side.
BEKIM: *v.t.*, recompense, pay back, give back, return, avenge, reply.
BEKPAUDA: *n.*, baking powder.
BEKLAIN: (Naut.): *n.*, rope running from masthead to stern; also rope capable of being used for that purpose.
BEKSAIT: *n.*, back (anat.), rear, back. Not buttocks.
BEL: *n.*, abdomen, also believed to be seat of mind and emotions; belly; fuselage of aeroplane. GAT BEL: pregnant.
BELIHAT: *a.*, state of anger or lust aroused.
BELO: *n.*, bell; period of rest from work usually denoted by a signal.
BELO BEK: *n.*, signal to return to work; one o'clock.
BELO KAIKAI: *n.*, luncheon.
BEMBE: *n.*, butterfly.
BENGIM: *v.t.*, bang, bump.
BENIT: *n.*, bayonet.
BENSIN: *n.*, benzine.
BERANDA: *n.*, verandah, porch.
BET: *n.*, bed, deck of canoe, resting place, shelf.

BETEN: *v.i.*, give honour (beten long ...).
BETSEL: *n.*, canvas hammock, canvas stretcher bed.
BIA: *n.*, beer.
BIHAIN: *adv.*, later after, following, at the rear of.
BIK: *a.*, big.
BIKBEL: *n.*, fat man; toadfish.
BIKBOT: *n.*, large vessel.
BIKBUS: *n.*, jungle, virgin bush.
BIKDAUNBILO: *n.*, hold of a ship.
BIKGAN: *n.*, cannon, piece of ordnance.
BIKHET: *v.i.*, boast, talk arrogantly or insolently; *n.*, idle boaster, upstart.
BIKJUDS: *n.*, judge.
BIKKAMPANI: *n.*, New Guinea Gold or Bulolo Gold Dredging Co.
BIKMAUS: *v.i.*, shout, talk in a loud voice, protest loudly boast; *n.*, man of loud words and no deeds, skite; codfish.
BIKNAIT: *n.*, around midnight.
BIKNEM: *n.*, name of the whole area or district.
BIKPELA: *a.*, large, big, important, great, huge.
BIKPLES: *n.*, mainland.
BIKROT: *n.*, main road.
BIKSAN: *n.*, the hours around midday.
BIKSI: *n.*, angry sea.
BIKSOLWARA: *n.*, ocean.
BIKTAUN: *n.*, capital city, main town.
BILAS: *v.i.*, show off, be conceited; put on ceremonial dress, ornaments or decorations; *a.*, flash, conceited, dressed or decorated; *n.*, ornaments or decorations. TOK BILAS- mockery, boasting.
BILASIM: *v.t.*, decorate, paint or deck with ornaments.
BILINAT: *n.*, betel nut; also the tree – family *palma, areca catechu* and *areca macrocarpa* – a tall slender palm with hard palmate branches and cluster of nuts about 2.5 cms long. Cultivated by the natives in coastal areas. Also called BUAI.
BILIP: *n.*, belief (miss).
BILIPIM: *v.t.*, believe in.
BILO: *n.*, half coconut shell used as a cup, dipper, ladle or bailer for canoes.
BILOIM: *v.t.*, bail (canoe).
BILONG: *v.i.*, be part of, be characterized by, be owned by; *conj.*, for the purpose of, because, on account of: *prep.*, of, for. *Vide* grammar, p.7.
BILONGEM: poss. pronoun, 3rd person; follows object possessed.
BILUM: *n.*, net bag.
BIN: auxiliary verb to form Past Perfect Indicative.
BIN: *n.*, bean. HASBIN- wing bean.

BINATANG: *n.*, generic term for insects.
BINEN: *n.*, honey bee.
BIPI: *n.*, Burns Philp. (Distinguish between this and PIPI.)
BIPO: *adv.*, before, in the past.
BIPOTAIM: *adv.*, once upon a time, formerly; *n.*, the past.
BIRUA: *n.*, death by violence, violent homicide. BIRUA LONG *v.t.*, assasinate, raid and slaughter.
BIS: *n.*, beads.
BISKIT: *n.*, biscuit.
BISNIS: *n.*, living or trade; responsibility.
BISOP: *n.*, bishop.
BIUGEL: *n.*, trumpet, bugle.
BLAISIM: *v.t.*, splice.
BLAK: *a.*, black
BLAK BOKIS: *n.*, flying fox; LIKLIK BLAK BOKIS- bat.
BLAK MISIN: *n.*, native mission helper.
BLAKPELA: *a.*, black.
BLAK KOKI: *n.*, black cockatoo.
BLAKSKIN: *n.*, black people.
BLANGKET: *n.*, blanket.
BLATIFUL: *n.*, bloody fool.
BLESIM: *v.t.*, bless.
BLOK: *n.*, pulley block.
BLOKIM: *v.t.*, block as in boxing.
BLU: *a.*, blue.
BLUPELA: *a.*, blue.
BLUPELA PIS: *n.*, blue parrot-fish about 30 cms long.
BLUT: *n.*, blood sap, glue. KARIM BLUT- menstruate.
BOA: *n.*, drill, auger; *v.t.*, BORIM.
BOI: *n.*, indentured labourer, native servant.
BOILIM: *v.t.*, boil.
BOINIM: *v.t.*, burn, wound or graze with a bullet.
BOKIS: *n.*, box; vagina; square boxlike fish about 23 cms long which inflates itself when danger is imminent; coffin. See TOK BOKIS p.115.
BOKIS AIN: *n.*, iron dispatch box.
BOKIS AIS: *n.*, ice chest.
BOKIS KAIKAI: *n.*, food safe or box.
BOKIS LAM: *n.*, lamp box.
BOKIS MARASIN: *n.*, medicine chest.
BOKIS MUSIK: *n.*, gramophone.
BOKIS PIKSA: *n.*, camera.
BOKSIN: *n.*, boxing, boxing gloves.

BOL: *n.,* scrotum, lead, bullet.

BOMBOM: *n.,* coconut palm frond; *v.i.,* fish with bombom torches; *v.t.,* BOMBOMIM.

BONAN: *n.,* two narrow oblique muscles behind the kidney and inside the abdominal cavity.

BONON: *n.,* dugong (also BULMAKAU BILONG SOLWARA).

BORIM: *.v.t.,* drill, bore.

BOSAI: *n.,* bullseye.

BOSBOI: *n.,* native foreman in charge of group of natives.

BOSIM: *n.,* be in charge of (men or things), have the care of.

BOSKRU: *n.,* crew.

BOT: *n.,* boat.

BOTOL: *n.,* bottle, obsidian.

BOTOLWARA: *n.,* water bottle. BOTOL WARA is a bottle of water.

BRAIDEL: *n.,* bridle.

BRAS: *n.,* brass buckles, etc., on police uniform, brassware.

BRASBEN: *n.,* haversack.

BRATA: *n.,* relative of same generation and same sex (can be either a male or a female); also friendly term of address.

BRET: *n.,* bread.

BRINGIM: *v.t.,* take along, lead or conduct, fetch, bring (word or news).

BRIS: *n.,* bridge, pier or wharf.

BRIS KANDA: *n.,* cane suspension bridge.

BROS: *n.,* brush, chest.

BROSIM: *v.t.,* brush.

BRUK: *a.,* broken; *v.i.,* break.

BRUKIM: *v.t.,* break, fold, dig or cut (ground).

BRUM: *n.,* broom.

BRUMIM: *v.t.,* sweep, round up.

BRUS: *n.,* leaf tobacco, cigar.

BUAI: *n.,* betel nut, betel nut palm; see BILINAT.

BUK: *n.,* boil, knot, lump, notch; book.

BUK TAMBU: *n.,* Bible.

BULMAKAU: *n.,* cow, bullock, beef; B. BILONG SOLWARA- dugong.

BUM (Naut.): *n.,* long pole to extend the bottom of a sail; boom.

BUN: *n.,* bone, rib of coconut leaf.

BUNARA: *n.,* an archer's bow.

BUNATING: *a.,* emaciated.

BUNG: *n.,* meeting or gathering, market; *v.i.,* gather together, flock, congregate.

BUNGIM: *v.t.,* put in one heap, make a pile, collect together.

BUS: *n.,* the bush. BUS KANAKA- a savage.

DAI: *n.,* death.
DAI: *v.i.,* referring to past means to die - LONGTAIM I DAI NAU;
     faint; (of engines) cease; (of lamps or fire) be extinguished:
     TOK I DAI NAU- matter to be regarded as settled, no more
     argument; become anaesthetized.
DAI LONG: *v.t.,* to want badly, long for, yearn after.
DAI PINIS: *v.i.,* die, died.
DAINAMAIT: *n.,* dynamite. Also PATRON.
DAKA: *n.,* green coloured fruit of the samll pepper vine *(piper betel).* It is
     hard, about the thickness of a pencil and 5 to 10 centimetres
     long. It is chewed with betel nut and is peppery in taste.
DAN: *a.,* cooked. NO DAN- uncooked, raw.
DANGIL: *n.,* mackerel.
DAUN: *adv.,* below, underneath, down. PLES DAUN- the Earth.
DAUNBILO: *adv.,* down below, below.
DAUNIM: *v.t.,* swallow, put down, knock (an opponent) down.
DE: *n.,* day.
DEO: *prop.n.,* God.
DEVEL: *n.,* soul, shadow, reflection, image.
DEVEL TAKONDO: *prop.n.,* Holy Spirit.
DIDIMAN: *n.,* Department of Agriculture; field staff of same.
DILIM: *v.t.,* divide out; apportion.
DINAUR: *n.,* debt, obligation; *v.t.,* DINAUR LONG- owe.
DIP: *n.,* dipping halyard on top gaff of a sail.
DISEL: *n.,* diesoline.
DISPELA: *dem.a.,* this.
DISI: *n.,* District Commissioner.
DIWAI: *n.,* any wood; generic name for trees.
DIWAI KROS: *n.,* Christian cross; crossed spars that hold boom and
     furled sail on boat deck.
DOK: *n.,* dog.
DOKOROK: *n.,* frog.
DOKTA: *n.,* medical officer, medical assistant; striped fish about
     15 cms long.
DONKI: *n.,* donkey, mule.
DOTI: *a.,* soiled, unclean; *n.,* hair, spittle, finger- and toenails, excreta,
     part of intimate clothing or scraps of tasted food - all these are
     referred to as DOTI when they are used to bewitch the person
     who owns them.
DOTI TUMAS: *a.,* filthy.
DRAI: *n.,* ripe coconut; *a.,* dry, withered.
DRAIDOK: *n.,* slipway for boats.
DRAIPELA: *a.,* mature, very big, huge.

DRAIWARA: *n.,* low tide.
DRAIWABOI: *n.,* driver. Now mostly DRAIVA.
DRIMAN: *v.i.,* dream.
DRINGK: *v.i.,* drink; *n.,* drink. DRINGKIM: *v.t.,* drink, inhale.
DRIP: *v.i.,* float, drift; *n.,* newly-formed coconut; heart, inner self.
DUA: *n.,* door, gate.
DUIM: *v.t.,* rape.

EKLESIA: *n.,* the Church.
EKSTRIMUNSKIO: *n.,* the Last Sacrament.
ELEVASIO: *n.,* the part of the Mass known as the Elevation.
EM: *pron.,* he, they, she, it, him, her, them.
ENSIN: *n.,* engine, machine, motor.
ENSINI: *n.,* engineer, mechanic.
EPA: *n.,* stingray, sunfish – *manta berostis*.
ERIMA: *n.,* large tree (*Octomeles sumatrana*), medium hardwood of light brown to greyish yellow colour.
ESEL: *n.,* mule, donkey.
ESIK: *n.,* vinegar.

FAIL: *n.,* file, rasp.
FAILIM: *v.t.,* file, rasp.
FAULNABAUT: *v.i.,* (of rumour, testimony, etc.), be conflicting, be contradictory; of rope, fishlines – become tangled.
FIKAS: *n.,* fig tree.
FIVA: *n.,* malaria, fever.
FRAIDE: *n.,* Friday.
FUT: *n.,* foot.

GABEL: *n.,* fork, gardening fork.
GALIMBONG: *n.,* sheath around the blossoms of the coconut tree.
GALIP: *n.,* small egg-shaped edible nut, about 5 centimetres long, produced on a large tree *(Canarium Polyphyllum)*. South Seas or Tahitian almond. G. BILONG GIRAUN- peanut.
GAM: *n.,* large clam, *melo amphora* and *m. ethiopicus,* bailer shell. Also GAMSEL.
GAN MASIN: *n.,* machine gun.
GAN PISIN: *n.,* shotgun.
GARAMUT: *n.,* a hollowed tree trunk used as a drum, or to send messages: a useful timber tree, *vitex cofassus*.
GAT: *v.t.,* have, possess; *n.,* police or military guard, squad.
GATEN: *n.,* garden (not usual) *vide* WOK.
GAVMAN: *n.,* Government, Administration, governor.
GEN: *adv.,* again, once more, despite it, nevertheless. See p.20.

GERAP: *v.i.*, rise; imper. get up! (See KALAP.)
GERAPIM: *v.t.*, waken; organise (dance, play, etc.).
GERAP NOGUT: *v.i.*, (fig.), start up in anger, fear or surprise; protest violently.
GIAMAN: *n.*, untrue or incorrect statement or account, lie, pretence, subterfuge; *a.*, make believe, not real, pretended; *v.i.*, misquote, lie, make an incorrect or inaccurate statement, make believe, feint, give mistaken information; pretend.
MAN BILONG GIAMAN- liar.
GIAMANIM: *v.t.*, mislead, deceive, impose on, give a wrong account to (someone), feint at.
GIRIGIRI: *n.*, small cowrie shell – *cypraea moneta moneta* and *cypraea moneta annulus* – used as currency and decoration.
GITA: *n.*, guitar, ukelele.
GIVIM: *v.t.*, give.
GLAS: *n.*, glass tumbler, anything glass.
GLAS BILONG AI: *n.*, spectacles. Also AI GLAS.
GLASIM: *v.t.*, fish with the aid of diving glasses; watch through telescope or glasses.
GLAS LUKLUK: *n.*, mirror.
GO: *v.i.*, go, go away.
GO APIM: *v.t.*, climb, mount, perform sexual act on.
GO HET (Naut.): *v.i.*, go ahead.
GO KAMAP: *v.i.*, go and arrive at destination, arrive at.
GO KAMBAUT: *v.i.*, travel in or about, wander about, peregrinate; habitate.
GOLIP: *n.*, pearl shell *(pinctada maxima)*.
GOLMESA: *n.*, sergeant major.
GOLMONI: *n.*, gold.
GORAUN: *v.i.*, sink, go down, descent, subside.
GORGOR: *n.*, *alpinia* sp., family *zingiberaceae,* an aromatic plant growing about 1.8 metres high and frequently used in magic and spells.
GORS: *n.*, antiseptic gauze, also metal gauze.
GOSTAN: *v.i.*, reverse.
GOT: *prop.n.*, God.
GRANAS: *n.*, coral and shell rubble.
GRAS: *n.*, hair, fur, feathers. GRAS BILONG LEK (slang) – "millions of 'em".
GRASIA: *n.*, grace (miss).
GRAUN: *n.*, ground, soil, the earth.
GREWE: *n.*, gravy.
GRILE: *n.*, skin infection in which patches of skin dry and scale off, ringworm *(Tinea Imbricata* and *t. annulata)*.

GRIS: *n.*, fat, dripping; suave talk; grease or vaseline; persuasion; ointment; *v.i.,* to chat or gossip in a friendly fashion.
GRISIM: *v.t.,* talk suavely to, ingratiate oneself with, inveigle, artfully persuade; lubricate.
GRIS KASKAS: *n.,* sulphur ointment, ointment for treatment of scabies.
GUDE: good day – a term of greeting.
GUMI: *n.,* rubber, rubber tube.
GURIA: *n.,* earth tremor, tremor; goura pigeon; *v.i.,* shake, tremble, quake, shiver; be nervous.
GUT: *adv.,* well.
GUTAIM: *n.,* peace, calm, good old days.
GUTBAI: goodbye.
GUTPELA: *a.,* good, tasty, upright, kind, just.

HAISIM: *v.t.,* lift, hoist.
HAIT: *v.i.,* to conceal oneself, be hidden, be unrevealed.
HAITIM: *v.t.,* conceal (person, thing or information).
HAIWARA: *n.,* high tide.
HALIAS: *n.,* halyard.
HALPIM: *v.t.,* relieve, replace; aid, help.
HAMA: *n.,* hammer.
HAMAMAS: *v.i.,* rejoice, be happy: HAMAMAS LONG- priase, speak well of, honour.
HAMARIM: *v.t.,* thrash or beat soundly.
HAMBAK: *v.i.,* trifle, make love, procrastinate, be aimless, sulk, play up; *n.,* waywardness, stubbornness.
HAN: *n.,* arm, limb of tree, paw.
HANGGIMAP: *v.i.,* be suspended.
HANGGIMAPIM: *v.t.,* hang, suspend or hang up.
HANGGRE: *a.,* hungry, greedy, feeling the lack of food; *n.,* shortage of food, hunger; e.g., TAIM BILONG HANGGRE- period between crops.
HANI: *n.,* honey.
HAN KAIS: *n.,* left hand; HAN SIUT: *n.,* right hand; HANWAS- wristwatch.
HANKAS: *n.,* handcuffs.
HAP: *n.,* portion; district or geographical or tribal area; *adv.,* there, in that place.
HAP GRAUN: *n.,* portion of land or country.
HAP HAPIM: *v.t.,* divide into two equal parts.
HAPIM: *v.t.,* divide into parts or portions.
HAPKAS: *n.,* light skinned native, man of mixed European and native blood, dark skinned European (Italian, Spanish, etc.).
HAPMAK: *n.,* sixpence, five cents, five toea.

HAP PISIN: *a.,* and *n.,* belonging to same group or association of clans.
HAPSAIT: *n.,* opposite or other side, further side.
HAPTUMARA: *adv.,* day after tomorrow.
HAPTUMARA MOA: 2nd day after tomorrow.
HAPTUMARA MOA YET: 3rd day after tomorrow.
HARIAP: *v.i.,* hurry; *imp.,* hurry up!
HARIM: *v.i.,* listen, think or consider; *v.t.,* hear, remember, hear tell
 of heed; HARIM LONG BEL- try to recall.
HASBIN: *n.,* wing bean.
HASKIM: *v.t.,* ask, question; HASKIM LIVA- think well, recollect.
HAT: *n.,* hat, cap.
HAT WOK: *v.i.,* perform an exacting task or duty, labour, undergo
 hardship in performance of a duty.
HAUMAS?: *adv.,* how many? how much?
HAUMAS DE?: What is the date?
HAUMAS KLOK?: What is the time?
HAUS: *n.,* house, building, shed, nest, dwelling.
HAUS AIS: *n.,* freezer.
HAUS BOI: *n.,* men's quarters or house in a village, indentured labourers'
 sleeping quarters.
HAUS DRING: *n.,* hotel.
HAUS KAIKAI: *n.,* mess, eating house, dining room.
HAUS KAPA: *n.,* house or building with an iron roof.
HAUS KIAP: *n.,* government rest house, a Kiap's house.
HAUS KOT: *n.,* court house.
HAUS KUK: *n.,* kitchen, cookhouse.
HAUS KUNAI: *n.,* house or building of grass.
HAUS LOTU: *n.,* church, house of worship.
HAUS MARIT: *n.,* house belonging to married couple.
HAUS MASIN: *n.,* engine room or shed.
HAUS MERI: *n.,* native women's house or sleeping quarters.
HAUS MISIN: *n.,* mission house, missionary's rest house in a village.
HAUS MONI: *n.,* bank; strongroom, house or room where cash
 transactions take place.
HAUS MOTAKAR: *n.,* garage.
HAUS PAMUK: *n.,* brothel.
HAUS PAUL: *n.,* fowlhouse.
HAUS PEPA: *n.,* District Office, office.
HAUS PEKPEK: *n.,* latrine, toilet closet, privy.
HAUS POLIS: *n.,* police barracks, police sleeping quarters.
HAUS POS: *n.,* post office.
HAUS SAKSAK: *n.,* building thatched with saksak fronds.
HAUS SEL: *n.,* tent.

HAUS SIK: *n.,* hospital.
HAUS SMOK: *n.,* copra drier.
HAUS WASWAS: *n.,* bathroom, bath house.
HAUSAT: *interrog.,* why? For what reason?
HEBSEN: *n.,* peas.
HET: *n.,* head; used metaphorically means authority or licence.
HET I PEN: *n.,* headache.
HETMAN: *n.,* "hat wearer", i.e., a Luluai, Tultul or Medical Tultul.
HETWIN: *n.,* head wind.
HEVE: *a.,* heavy, weighty, clumsy, unpractised; *n.,* weight.
HEVEN: *n.,* Heaven.
HIA: *adv.,* here, in this place; *dem. a.,* this.
HIP: *n.,* disordered collection, scattered collection.
HIPAREI: *n.,* cheering, acclamation; *v.i.,* cheer.
HIPIM: *v.t.,* throw together indiscriminately or without order.
HIP NABAUT: *a.,* scattered, lying about in disorder.
HOBEL: *n.,* plane.
HOISALO!: *imp.,* all together, up!
HOLAN: *v.i.,* wait! stop a minute!
HOLIM: *v.t.,* hold, handle.
HOLIM PAS: *v.t.,* arrest, seize and hold.
HOS: *n.,* horse.
HOT, HOTPELA: *a.,* hot, strict, severe; *colloq.,* terrific!
HOT GRIS: *n.,* antiphlogistine or poulticine.
HOTPELA: *a.,* vigorous; also *excl.,* "Hot Stuff!"
HOT WARA: *n.,* hot water.
HUK: *n.,* fish hook, hook; *v.i.,* (MI GO HUK).
HUKIM: *v.t.,* catch with line and hook; strike fiercely with hand or rod for discipline
HUL: *n.,* hole, excavation.
HUM: *n.,* family *pandanaceae.* Leaves long and fleshy and often used for walls of native huts. Fruit not edible.
HUSAT: *pron.,* interrogative who? whom?; *rel.,* who, whom; BILONG HUSAT?- whose?

I: a predicate marker in a clause or sentence, e.g., EM I GO – he goes. See p.12 "Word boundaries".
IMPERNO: *n.,* hell.
INAP: *a.,* equal, sufficient, suitable; NO INAP- too big, unsuitable, insufficient; INAP LONG- until.
INAPIM: *v.t.,* divide and give sufficient to each.
INDULGENSIA: *n.,* indulgences (miss).
INGK: *n.,* ink.
INGGLIS: *n.,* and *a.,* English or British.

INSAIT: *adv.,* inside, within, immersed in; *n.,* inside; INSAIT LONG- in, into, under; INSAIT LONG WARA- under the water (see NISAIT).
IROTU: *n.,* see KALAPLIM.
ISI: *a.,* not difficult, gentle; *adv.,* gently, smoothly, carefully, quietly.

JUDA: *prop.n.,* Jew.
JULAI: *n.,* July.
JUN: *n.,* June.

KABIS: *n.,* cabbage.
KAGO: *n.,* baggage, cargo, supplies.
KAGOBOI: *n.,* native carrier.
KAIKAI: *n.,* food, meal, feast; *v.i.,* eat, have a meal; *v.t.,* eat, bite, chew, swallow, envelope, corrode.
KAIN: *n.,* sort, kind, example.
KAIS: *a.,* left; *adv.,* left side.
KAISIM: *v.t.,* aim or direct to the left, hit left of target.
KAKALAK: *n.,* cockroach; also KOKOROS.
KAKARIM: *v.t.,* give birth to.
KAKI: *a.,* khaki.
KALABUS: *n.,* gaol, prison or house of detention, prisoner. Also a MAL. *q.v.* Net of ship's sling to hoist cargo; sling in which stones are carried away from mining face.
KALABUSIM: *v.t.,* imprison, forcibly seclude, shut in.
KALAP: *v.i.,* leap, leap up, jump or bound, escape.
KALAPIM: *v.t.,* leap, vault or scramble over. Cross over (as a river), board a ship or vehicle. KALAP LONG-
KALAP NOGUT: *v.i., (fig.)* start up in anger, fear, surprise; protest violently. Also GERAP NOGUT.
KALAPILIM: *n.,* large, branching coastal tree with picturesque foliage of dark green leaves. *(Calophyllum sp.)*; also known as IROTU.
KALOPA: *n.,* object of pity or sympathy; *a.,* pitiable, worthy of sympathy.
KALUK: *n.,* wooden headrest or "pillow".
KAM: *v.i.,* come; *imp.,* come. KAM WE?- where did you (he, etc.) come from?
KAMANGORO: *n.,* a tree growing to about 12 metres and with greyish-green bark marked by annular ridges up its trunk where branches have been cast off during growth. Leaves are oblate and about 20 cms by 7 cms. The young leaf shoots are edible. Also known as TULIP.
KAMAP: *v.i.,* arrive, approach, be revealed, happen or take place, eventuate.
KAMDA: *n.,* carpenter; W.R. Carpenter & Co. Ltd.

KAM DAUN: *v.i.*, descend towards.

KAM KAMAP: *v.i.*, arrive eventually or at last, arrived at.

KAMNDA: *n.*, carpenter; (K.)- W.R. Carpenter & Co. Ltd.

KAMPANG: *n.*, betel lime, lime, talc, whitewash.

KAMPANG SMEL: *n.*, scented talc or powder.

KAMPANI: *n.*, one not associated with mission or government; trader, man in private business, business house or association.

KAMPAS: *n.*, navigating compass, prismatic compass.

KAMDABOI: *n.*, a native carpenter, native who assists a carpenter.

KAN: *n.*, female external genitals.

KANAI: *n.*, seagull.

KANAKA: *n.*, free native, native in his village.

KANDA: *n.*, rattan cane (*calamus* spp.); walking stick of cane; *a.*, made of cane.

KANDEL: *n.*, candle.

KANDERE: *n.*, maternal uncle, and nephews and nieces of same.

KANDEREMAN: *n.*, nephew. See p.161.

KANDIS: *n.*, canvas, webbing cartridge pouches.

KANGAL: *n.*, feathered headdress worn in ceremony.

KANGKO: *n.*, watercress.

KANON: *n.*, Canon of the Mass.

KANU: *n.*, canoe.

KAP: *n.*, cup; gaff or spar at top of mainsail.

KAPA: *n.*, iron or any metal, roofing iron, finger or toenail, fish scales.

KAPA RESA: *n.*, razor blade.

KAPIAK: *n.*, breadfruit; family *moraceae autocarpus integra*. A tall tree of striking appearance, lactate, and with large lobed leaves with foliar stipules. Flowers in clusters and fruit is collective and round – edible.

KAPOPO: *n.*, and *v.i.*, fart.

KAPSAIT: *v.i.*, capsize, turn over, spill.

KAPSAITIM: *v.t.*, spill, pour out, capsize, tip up, tip out.

KAPUL: *n.*, opossum, cuscus.

KARABAU: *n.*, buffalo.

KARAMAP: *n.*, covering; parcel, package.

KARAMAPIM: *v.t.*, cover, envelope. See KARAPAIM.

KARAPAIM: *v.t.*, hide, secrete, cover over, conceal; *n.*, parcel.

KARAPAI: *n.*, wild corn.

KARAPUA: *n.*, short and fat banana which is cooked.

KARASIN: *n.*, kerosene.

KARI: *n.*, curry.

KARIM: *v.t.*, carry, give birth to; also KAKARIM, KARIM BLUT- menstruate.

KARUA: *n.,* mullet.
KARUKA: *n.,* tree of family *pandaceae;* mat or covering made from same.
KAS: *n.,* barrel, keg or cask.
KASANG: *n.,* peanut.
KASAWEL: *n.,* castor oil.
KASKAS: *n.,* scabies, a scabious skin infection characterized by patches of small scabs. It is contagious and yields to treatment with a sulphur ointment.
KASTA: *n.,* custard; a nut *(Parinari Laurini)* containing an oil valuable for its drying properties. The tree is small to medium, about 1 metre girth and up to 9 metres high. The nut is hard, rough and woody, ovoid in shape. The shell of the nut is grated and used by the natives to caulk canoes and gum spear heads.
KASTANS: *n.,* Customs Office and Officer.
KAT: *n.,* playing cards.
KATA: *n.,* launch or cutter.
KATIM: *v.t.,* cut, amputate, castrate (bol), circumcise (kok), carve.
KATOLIK: *n.,* Catholic.
KATRIS: *n.,* cartridge.
KATU: *n.,* hermit crab.
KAUKAU: *n., ipomea batatus;* sweet potato of which several varieties are grown in the Territory.
KAUL: *n.,* species of bamboo with thin-walled stems, sparsely leafed with a hair-like fringe at each nodule.
KAUNTIM: *v.t.,* read, enumerate, count.
KAUNTIM AUT: *v.t.,* read aloud, spell out.
KAUWAS: *n.,* friend, friendly term of address (Manus).
KAWAWAR: *n.,* wild ginger. Family *zingerberaceae.*
KAWIWI: *n.,* wild variety of betel nut. Nuts are smaller and more acrid than the cultivated variety and the tree is found far inland. Family *palmae,* genus *howea belmoreana.*
KEK: *n.,* cake.
KELA: *n.,* and *a.,* baldheaded.
KEMPE: *n.,* leprosy. See TOMATA.
KEN: *v.aux.,* can, be able.
KEPOK : *n.,* cotton wool, kapok, kapok tree.
KEPSTAN: *n.,* cut tobacco bought in tin or packet.
KEPTEN: *n.,* captain, air pilot, man in charge of boat.
KEROSEN: *n.,* kerosene.
KES: *n.,* wooden box or case, cage, coop.
KETEL: *n.,* kettle, teapot.
KI: *n.,* key, spanner.
KIAP: *n.,* magistrate, Patrol Officer, members of the Court of Native Affairs.

KIAU: *n.,* egg, torch bulb, electric light globe, testicle. MATA KIAU- having one eye.
KIDNI: *n.,* kidney.
KIK: *n.,* recoil (of a gun or rifle), *v.i.,* kick.
KIKBAL: *n.,* soccer football; *v.i.,* play football.
KIKBEK: *n.,* canvas swag bag, kitbag.
KIKIM: *v.t.,* pedal, kick.
KIKROS: *n.,* football match the outcome of a challenge; *v.i.,* play same.
KIL: *n.,* keel, sharp mountain ridge, roof ridge.
KILIM: *v.t.,* strike with a weapon or instrument: give great pain to.
KILMAN: *n.,* murderer.
KINA: *n.,* oyster.
KINDAM: *n.,* prawn, shrimp, lobster, crayfish.
KING: *n.,* king.
KININ: *n.,* quinine.
KININ WARA: *n.,* quinine water.
KINYA: *n.,* pearl-shell, mussel.
KIPAP: *v.i.,* to tack close to the wind, keep up to the wind.
KISIM: *v.t.,* fetch, obtain, get.
KIT: *n.,* putty.
KIVUNG: *n.,* Council of Elders; meeting.
KIWI: *n.,* boot or leather polish.
KLAMBU: *n.,* mosquito net, small net.
KLAMSEL: *n.,* all varieties of clams and mussels.
KLANGAL: *n.,* large dark red and blue or green parrot.
KLAUT: *n.,* cloud. KLAUT I PAS- overcast. KLAUT I LAIT- lightning.
KLIARIM: *v.t.* clear.
KLIA: *v.imp.,* make way! stand back! clear out! *a.,* standing clear, cleared.
KLIN: *a.,* clean, smooth, fresh.
KLINIM: *v.t.,* clean, tidy, make smooth.
KLINPELA: *a.,* same as klin above but needs a noun to follow it.
KLIWA: *n.,* jib, triangular foremast sail.
KLOK: *n.,* clock.
KLOS: *n.,* woman's blouse; clothes, dress; "Mother Hubbard".
KLOSAP: *adv.,* nearly, almost.
KLOS SINGSING: *n.,* formal clothes.
KLOS SLIP: *n.,* pyjamas.
KLOSTU: *a.,* near, nearby, not far.
KOK: *n.,* penis.
KOKI: *n.,* cockatoo.
KOKO: *n.,* cocoa.
KOKOMO: *n.,* hornbill.
KOKONAS: *n.,* coconut tree, coconut. See DRAI, DRIP, KULAU.

KOKOROS: *n.,* cockroach. See also **KAKALAK**.
KOKORUK: *n.,* domestic fowls. K. MAN- rooster.
KOL: *n.,* and *a.,* damp, cold; dew. PLES KOL- shade.
KOLIM: *v.t.,* name, designate, impute.
KOL KAIKAI: *n.,* food generally eaten cold, *i.e.,* ham, beetroot, etc.
KOLSINGLIS: *n.,* guernsey, sweater.
KOLSIS: *n.,* coastal hardwood tree like a mangrove.
KOL SISEL : *n.,* a cold chisel for ironwork.
KOL TA: *n.,* tar, creosote.
KOLWIN: *n.,* sea breeze.
KOM: *n.,* large white cowrie *(cypraea ovula)*; comb; cow's horn.
KOMUNIO: *n.,* Holy Communion.
KON: *n.,* corn.
KONA: *n.,* corner.
KONDA: *a.,* Treasury note, paper money.
KONFESSIO: *n.,* Sacrament of Confession.
KONGKONG: *n.,* Chinaman; *a.,* Chinese (not considered courteous now – see **SAINA**); also slang for "adze".
KONSEKRASIO: *n.,* part of the Mass known as the Consecration.
KONTRAK: *n.,* contract of service.
KOPIRUL: *n.,* corporal in the Native Constabulary or P.I.R.
KOPIS KRISTI: *n.,* Corpus Christi.
KOPRA: *n.,* dried meat of the coconut from which the oil is expressed.
KOR: *n.,* heart (miss.).
KORAKUM: *n.,* small red ant about 13 mms long that preys on insect larvae and is a valuable pest destroyer on coconut plantations.
KORVO: *n.,* stingray.
KOR-YESUS: *n.,* Sacred Heart of Jesus.
KOT: *n.,* court, action at law; *v.i.,* bring a complaint to a magistrate or the police.
KOTIM: *v.t.,* bring a person before the court.
KOTKOT: *n.,* crow, raven.
KOT REN: *n.,* raincoat.
KRAI: *v.i.,* weep; (of animals, birds) call, cry; *n.,* cry or call (of animals, birds). KRAI LONG- long for, yearn after.
KRAIDE: *n.,* chalk or limestone. See **SOK**.
KRAIKRAI: *v.i.,* weep copiously.
KRAKON: *n.,* rope obtained from a long thin bush vine.
KRANAS: *n.,* coral rubble.
KRANI: *n.,* Malay.
KRANKI: *n.,* foolishness, stupidity; *a.,* foolish, indiscreet, unwise; wrong.
KRANKINABAUT: *v.i.,* acting foolishly.
KRIKET: *n.,* cricket.

KRISMAS: *n.,* Christmas.

KROBA: *n.,* crowbar, steel bar.

KRONGUT: *v.i.,* bend.

KRONGUTIM: *v.t.,* stub foot against, knock against, bend or curve.

KROPELA: *n.,* propeller, ship's screw.

KROPIS: *n.,* crayfish.

KROS: *a.,* angry, annoyed; *n.,* anger. DIWAI KROS- Christian Cross; also bipod rigged on deck to hold boom and sails when furled.

KROSIM: *v.t.,* reprimand, scold.

KRU: *n.,* brain, mushroom, shoot, vital meat of a seed which feeds the nascent shoot, a nursery coconut ready for planting.

KRUTMAN: *n.,* recruit.

KUK: *n.,* cook, art of cooking, wife; a game of cards; PLE KUK- to play KUK; *v.i.,* cook. KUKA: *n.,* crab.

KUKAMBA: *n.,* cucumber.

KUKBOI: *n.,* native cook, cookboy. (Starting to go out out of fashion.)

KUKEN: *n.,* small cake.

KUKIM: *v.t.,* cook, burn or consume with fire.

KUKURAI: *n.,* Head man or chief, same as LULUAI, but is sometimes used for a head man not formally appointed.

KULAU: *n.,* green coconut, from which is obtained a refreshing drink.

KUMU: *n.,* general term for edible leaves. Also SAIOR.

KUMUL: *n.,* bird of paradise.

KUMURERE: *n.,* large tree of striking appearance and with large light green foliage. It is not heavily foliaged; *Eucalyptus deglupta.*

KUNAI: *n.,* lalang grass; *imperata arundinacea* – tough, long bladed grass growing as high as 1.8 metres and common in the Territory, high cellulose content.

KUNDAR: *n.,* altar boy.

KUNDU: *n.,* native drum. It is shaped like an hourglass and has an animal or a reptile skin taut over one end. It is beaten with the hand.

KURKURUA: *n.,* rosary beads.

KUS: *n.,* and *v.i.,* cough.

KUSKUS: *n.,* clerk, secretary.

KUS MARASIN : *n.,* cough mixture.

KWIK: *adv.,* quickly.

KWIKTAIM: *adv.,* quickly, speedily.

KWILA: *n.,* large hardwood tree – *afzelia (Intsia) bijuga* – the wood is very durable.

KWIN: *n.,* queen, Virgin Mary.

LAIK: *v.i.,* be willing; *aux.v.,* to indicate immediate future, *i.e.,* about to do something; *v.t.,* and followed by a pronoun and verb to mean desire or intention to do something. *Vide* grammar; *n.,* wish or desire.

LAIKIM: *v.t.,* like, desire, wish for. *Vide* grammar. LAIKIM TUMAS- love.

LAIM: *n.,* glue; *v.t.,* LAIMIM.

LAIN: *v.i.,* arrange (themselves) in order, make a line, line for inspection; *n.,* clan.

LAINIM: *v.t.,* teach, tutor, arrange in a line for inspection, set (a table), align.

LAIT: *v.i.,* shine, glitter, glow, shed light, take fire, light.

LAITIM: *v.t.,* light.

LAKA?: *interrog.,* understand? Am I not right? Is it not? Follow me?

LALA: *n.,* species of shoal fish.

LALAI: *n.,* trochus shell.

LAM: *n.,* lamp.

LAM BENSIN: *n.,* primus lamp.

LAM WOKABAUT: *n.,* hurricane lamp.

LANG: *n.,* housefly, fly.

LANGSAM: *v.i.,* go slow, dawdle.

LANGUL: *n.,* a large fish of the trevally family.

LANIS: *n.,* towboat, whaleboat.

LAP: *v.i.,* laugh, chuckle, smile. BILONG LAP- funny.

LAPAP: (Naut.) *v.i.,* luff up.

LAPLAP: *n.,* lavalava or length of cloth worn around the waist like a kilt, cloth material of any sort.

LAPUN: *a.,* aged; *n.,* old person.

LARIM: *v.t.,* let off punishment, don't disturb, *e.g.,* larim i stap; let him go.

LAS: *n.,* in gambling a last chance. When a player has won all the stakes he gives the others a LAS, that is a chance to win back what they lost by staking the winnings or the greater part of them to nothing for a final hand.

LATA: *n.,* stairs, steps, ladder.

LATAPIM: *v.t.,* wrap up.

LAULAU: *n.,* large dark green tree with small pear-shaped red fruit which are edible and have not much taste. Malay Apple – probably *Eugenia Malacensis* – makes a good pie with lemon juice and cinnamon.

LAUP : *n.,* New Guinea Walnut *(Dracontomelum Mangiferum)* tree, valuable for its timber.

LAUS: *n.,* flea.

LEGOIM: *v.t.,* release, drop, unhand. LEGOIM ANKA – drop the anchor.

LEK: *n.,* foot, leg, footprint. LEK BILONG WARA – river mouth.

LENS KOPIRUL: *n.,* lance corporal in the Native Constabulary.

LEPHAN: *adv.,* left side, left; *n.,* left hand.

LEPRA: *n.,* person afflicted with leprosy. See KEMPE and TOMATA.

LES: *v.i.,* be disinclined, be indolent, loaf, be blase, have no liking for, wash one's hands of. LES TUMAS- be very lazy.

LESMAN: *n.,* loafer.

LET: *n.,* belt, leather, leather goods.

LIK: *v.i.,* and *n.,* leak.

LIKLIK: *a.,* undersized, small, frail of stature, little; *n.,* small quantity or portion; thin, narrow; *adv.,* slightly.

LIKLIK DOKTA: *n.,* Medical Assistant.

LIKLIK MASKET: *n.,* pistol. Also HAN GUN.

LIMBOM: *n.,* tall, slender, hardwood palm – *kentiopsis archonto-phoenix*. The wood is used for spears, arrows, bows, floors, etc., by the natives.

LIMLIMBU: *n.,* leave, holiday, day off, recreation; *v.i.,* holiday, spend a day off; LIMLIMBU LONG ...- visit.

LING: *n.,* surgical lint.

LINTAUN: *v.i.,* stoop, bend down.

LIP: *n.,* leaf, foliage.

LIPIM: *v.t.,* leave, leave behind.

LIP TI: *n.,* tea leaves.

LITIMAPIM: *v.t.,* lift, take up.

LIVA: *n.,* liver and is thought to be the seat of the mind; ASKIM LIVA BILONG YU – think well (lit., "ask your liver"); WETLIVA- lung.

LO: *n.,* law, regulation, rule, custom.

LOK: *n.,* lock, padlock.

LOKIM: *v.t.,* bolt, lock.

LOMBO: *n.,* chillies, capsicum.

LONG: *prep.,* to, by, with, from, at, in, per, on, in regard to, in respect to. *Vide* grammar, p.22.

LONGLONG: *a.,* insane, mad, idiotic, subject to fits, confused.

LONGPELA: *a.,* lengthy, tall, long, rangy; LONGPELA NATING- tall and thin.

LONGPELA MAUS: *n.,* garfish.

LONGPELA NEK: *n.,* crane, heron.

LONGTAIM: *n.,* considerable period, long time. LONG TAIM means when, at the time when- .

LONGWE: *a.,* far, long, distant.

LORI: *n.,* truck, utility truck, motor lorry.

LOT: *n.,* roll (of cloth).

LOTIM: *v.t.,* roll up, coil.

LOTU: *n.,* church service; *v.i.,* attend church. HAUS LOTO- church.

LOTUIM: *v.t.,* worship.

LUKAUT!: *exclam.*, take care! beware! LUKAUT LONG- beware of.

LUKAUTIM: *v.t.*, guard, watch over, take care of, supervise. Search for is PAINIM.

LUKIM: *v.t.*, see, regard, look at, notice.

LUKLUK: *n.*, look, glance; *v.i.*, look.

LUKSAVE: *v.i.*, recognise, know by sight; LUKSAVE LONG ...

LULUAI: *n.*, head man or chief of a village so confirmed by the administration.

LUS: *a.*, lost, forgotten, left, dead.

LUSIM: *v.t.*, forget, leave behind, lose, leave; untie, unlock, take off (clothes).

MAGAU: *n.*, fish about 36 cms long, brown and feeds about reefs and rocks.

MAISEL: *n.*, chisel, KOL SISEL- cold chisel.

MAK: *n.*, sign, figure, mark, letter of the alphabet, pattern; 10 cents. KOLIM MAK- sound with the lead-line.

MAKAS: *n.*, small tree, flowers hibiscus type, yellow and reddish purple centre – *hibiscus filiaceus*.

MAKIM: *v.t.*, demonstrate, mark, figure, name a day or time.

MAL: *n.*, narrow strip of bark or strings and hanging from the belt to the knees so as to cover the pubes. It is worn by both sexes in some parts of N.G.

MALAMBUR: *n.*, herring.

MALIRA: *n.*, love spell. There are many forms, mostly performed by men. A common one is to say a spell over some aromatic or pungent smelling leaf, root or sap and give it to the victim in food, a cigarette, etc., where she (or he) becomes aware of it.

MALISA: *n.*, sea pike, barracuda.

MALO: *n.*, large white tree, family *ficus*, with numerous fruit springing from trunk and branches.

MALOLO: *v.i.*, and *n.*, rest, spell.

MAMA: *n.*, mother – classificatory and biological.

MAMAIT: *n.*, marmite, beef extract, vegetable extract.

MAMBU: *n.*, bamboo; *a.*, made of bamboo; also barrel of shotgun, long tube.

MAMI: *n.*, a tuber root vegetable somewhat similar to a yam and of same species (fam. *convolvulaceae, dioscorea* spp.).

MAN: *n.*, male, man, fellow; *a.*, male; also used as an exclamation.

MANDATO: *n.*, Commandment.

MANDE: *n.*, Monday.

MANG: *n.*, small, rat-like animal with long tail.

MANGAL: *a.*, admire but with some overtones of envy.

MANGGO: *n.*, mango; family *anocardiaceae* and edible, genus is usually *mangifera indica*. Wild variety is probably *mangifera odorata*.
MANGGROS: *n.*, mangroves – *rhizophora mucronata*, etc.
MANGKI: *n.*, male native child, native youth.
MANGKI MASTA: *n.*, male domestic servant, native valet.
MANIGULAI: *n.*, sea eagle; osprey.
MANMERI: *n.*, everybody.
MANOBUS: *n.*, savage, ignorant bush-dweller.
MANUWA: *n.*, warship. Also derisively- a fat man.
MARAMAL: *n.*, jacaranda tree.
MARASIN: *n.*, medicine, chemical.
MARIA: Mary, the Mother of Christ.
MARIMARI: *v.i.*, have mercy, pity; MARIMARI LONG ...
MARIO: *n.*, eel (freshwater).
MARIP: *n.*, small, red and green parrot.
MARIT: *a.*, married, joined, confluent; *n.*, marriage, married person.
MARITA: *n.*, tree of family *pandaceae*. Bears long conical collective fruit about 51 cms long. Is edible and cultivated by the natives. The fruit also is known as MARITA. Another variety has a spherical fruit with conical phalanges of wood tissue and sweet juice.
MARITIM: *v.t.*, marry.
MAROTA: *n.*, leaves of the Nipa palm used as thatch; nipa palm.
MAS: *n.*, mast, flagpole; *v.i.*, must; have to.
MASALAI: *n.*, the Devil, fiend, demon.
MASIN: *n.*, engine, machine. *Vide* HAUS MASIN.
MASIS: *n.*, matches, cigarette lighter.
MASKET: *n.*, gun or rifle.
MASKI: *adv.*, never mind, no matter, let be, don't bother.
MASKITA: *n.*, mosquito.
MASTA: *n.*, white man, employer, Mr.
MASTA KOT: *n.*, lawyer.
MASTA MAK: *n.*, surveyor.
MATAKIAU: *n.*, man blind in one eye; *a.*, with one eye.
MATMAT: *n.*, burial ground, cemetery.
MAU: *a.*, ripe.
MAUS: *n.*, mouth, opening, muzzle of firearm.
MAUSPAS: *a.*, dumb.
MAUNTEN: *n.*, hill, mountain.
ME: *n.*, goat.
MEME: *n.*, pith or unedible part of fruit, etc., wax or honeycomb; dregs.
MEKIM: *v.t.*, do, perform, render, cause, shake; MEKIM SAVE- teach a lesson. This phrase is used to "egg on" performers, players, and even labourers. It is a form of barracking.

MEKIM DAI: *v.t.,* kill; MEKIM DAI SKIN BILONGEN- commit suicide; (of engines) switch off; (of lamps or fire) extinguish.
MEKNAIS: *v.i.,* shake, vibrate, nod, wave, bob, rustle, rattle.
MEKPAS: *n.,* parcel, wrapped bundle.
MEK PEPA: *v.t.,* make a contract of service.
MELEK: *n.,* semen.
MELEN: *n.,* melon.
MELUM MELUM: *a.,* soft, pulpy, swampy.
MENDAL: *n.,* medal.
MENSEL: *n.,* mainsail.
MENSIT: *n.,* mainsheet.
MERI: *n.,* native woman, native's wife.
MI: *pron.,* I, me.
MIPELA: *pron.,* we, us. *Vide* grammar.
MISA: *n.,* the Mass.
MISIN: *n.,* mission, missionary.
MISINBOI: *n.,* native catechist teacher, mission helper.
MISIS: *n.,* white woman, white man's wife.
MIT: *n.,* flesh, muscle; MIT I DAI- become numbed.
MOA: *adv.,* very. *Vide* grammar- "Comparison of Adjectives". *n.,* some more.
MOABETA: *a.,* better, very good; MOABETA MI GO- I had better go.
MON: *n.,* high prowed canoe without an outrigger.
MONI: *n.,* money, wages.
MONINGTAIM: *n.,* morning.
MONKI: *n.,* monkey. *cf.* MANKI.
MORAN: *n.,* python, carpet snake.
MORSO: *n.,* species of reef fish.
MOSONG: *n.,* fine hairs, downy hairs.
MOTAKAR: *n.,* motor car.
MUKMUK: *n.,* a mottled black and white stone, round and flat, about the size of a saucer or smaller with a sharpened perimeter and pierced through the centre. The larger ones are the badge or mark of rank amongst the natives of south-west New Britain. The smaller ones were used for currency.
MULI: *n.,* lemon, lime.
MUMU: *n.,* a hole in the ground lined with banana leaves, filled about a third with very hot stones with a pad of banana leaves on them. The food is wrapped in banana or pawpaw leaves, placed in the MUMU, the liner leaves folded over and the earth filled in. The food is thus cooked under pressure and is very tender.
MUMUT: *a.,* concerned with town sanitary service; small marsupial or a rodent, somewhat bigger than a rat – probably a bandicoot. MUMUT LAIN is the sanitary gang.

MUMUTIM: *v.t.,* undermine, scavenge, root or dig under.
MUN: *n.,* moon, month; *v.i.,* pool monthly wages. It is a custom on many labour lines for a group of natives to pool their wages each month and each in turn take the monthly pool.
MURUK: *n.,* cassowary.
MUSIK: *n.,* mouth organ.

NA: *conj.,* and, now, or.
NABAUT: *adv.,* around about, indiscriminately.
NABAUT NABAUT: *adv.,* here and there, everywhere, all over the place, widely scattered.
NAINSI: *n.,* an effeminate man.
NAIP: *n.,* knife, sword. NAIP SKRU- penknife. NAIP BRET: *n.,* breadknife.
NAIT: *n.,* night.
NAMBA: *n.,* mark, lettering, letter of the alphabet, figures, number.
NAMBA TU : *a.,* ord. num.- second.
NAMBA WAN: *a.,* very good, excellent, principle, chief; ord. num. first; *n.,* chief one, principal.
NAMBIS: *n.,* beach, coast.
NAMEL: *n.,* middle, in between.
NANIS: *n.,* pineapple (also ANANAS, q.v.).
NARAKAIN: *n.,* indef. demon. – different, of another kind or species.
NARASAIT: *n.,* other side, opposite side.
NASAU: *n.,* a mild term of abuse, a dunderhead.
NATING: *adv.,* merely, only without purpose, and nothing more, and that's all. *Vide* grammar, p.20.
NATNAT: *n.,* midge, gnat, sandfly.
NAU: *adv.,* now, at this time.
NAU WONEM: indeed, of course, what otherwise?
NEK: *n.,* neck, throat. LONGPELA NEK- heron.
NEK I PAS: *a.,* dumb, see MAUSPAS.
NEM: *n.,* name, title, authority, reputation; GAT NEM LONG- be known for.
NGOS NGOS: *n.,* lice.
NI: *n.,* knee. Also SKRU.
NIL: *n.,* nail, needle, thorn, pin.
NILIM: *v.t.,* fasten with nails.
NINIK: *n.,* bee. See BINEN.
NISAIT: Same as INSAIT.
NIUSPEPA: *n.,* newspaper.
NO: *adv.,* not.
NOGAT: *v.t.,* neg., no (emphatic) by no means!
NO GAT: *v.t.,* have not, be without.
NO GUT: *a.,* bad, no good, unsuitable, spoilt, disturbed.
NO INAP: *a.,* too big, too long, too large, too much, unsuitable, too small.

NOK: *n.,* flower cluster of the coconut palm.
NO KEN: *v.i.,* be unable, cannot; strong negative.
NO LAIK: *v.i.,* be unwilling, disinclined, be undesirous.
NONG: *a.,* having nothing to say, stupidly silent.
NO SAVE: *v.i.,* be unacquainted with, not have any knowledge of, be unaccustomed.
NUBRIKEN: *n.,* New Britain.
NUKPUKU: *v.i.,* confess unreservedly, own up, make an unequivocable confession.
NUPELA: *a.,* new.
NUS: *n.,* nose.

OKARI: *n.,* a large nut-bearing tree of coastal Papua *(Terminalia Kaernbachii).* Also name for the nut which tastes like GALIP. See TALIS.
OL: *n.,* all, everyone; the indefinite "they".
OLABOI!: See OLAMAN!
OLAMAN!: *exclam.,* goodness!; by Jove! etc.
OLGETA: *a.,* all, every in a general sense; *adv.,* wholly, totally, absolutely.
OLMAN: *n.,* everybody.
OLSEM: *adv.,* so, thus, in this manner, in the manner of, similar to, like, after the style of.
OLPELA: *a.,* worn, not new, out of date, old (of things).
OLTAIM: *adv.,* always, constantly, all the time.
OP: *a.,* open; *v.i.,* open.
OPERTORIUM: *n.,* Offertory of the Mass.
OPIM: *v.i.,* open, separate, part.
OPIS: *n.,* office. See HAUS PEPA.
OPTIN: *n.,* tin opener.
ORAIT: *a.,* satisfactory, all right; *colloq.,* right ho!; *conj.,* so, well.
ORAITIM: *v.t.,* repair.
ORATAVO: *n.,* religious instruction.
ORAVASIO: *n.,* sermon.

PAIA: *n.,* fire; *a.,* alight, lit, burning; *v.i.,* catch alight, fire a gun.
PAIAWIN: *n.,* land breeze.
PAIAWUD: *n.,* firewood.
PAINIM: *v.t.,* search for, seek, meet, come upon.
PAINIM PINIS: *v.t.,* have found it.
PAINAP: *n.,* pineapple.
PAIP: *n.,* pipe, gun-barrel, piping; PAIP BILONG NEK- trachea.
PAIRAP: *v.i.,* explode, burst into flames, snap or crackle (sticks, twigs, etc., when walked on).
PAIT: *n.,* battle, quarrel, dissension, fight; *v.i.,* fight, quarrel.
PAITIM: *v.t.,* beat, thrash, mash, pound.

PAKIM: *v.t.,* to carnally know, commit sodomy on.

PAKIMHAS: *n.,* one who commits sodomy on another (see AISMALANG).

PALAI: *n.,* lizard, iguana.

PAL PAL: *n.,* medium-sized tree with large ternate leaves, hastate in shape and with yellow-white ribs. Branches are green and thorny and trunk is grey. Bears a round, nutlike fruit in a green case about 2 cms in diameter. It may grow to over 12 metres, though usually much smaller.

PAM: *n.,* pump, heart, piston, pulse.

PAMKEN: *n.,* pumpkin.

PAMLIL: *n.,* cobbler's palm.

PAMUK: *n.,* harlotry, prostitution; MERI PAMUK- harlot.

PANGAL: *n.,* stalk of the coconut frond.

PAPA: *n.,* father – biological and classificatory.

PAPAI: *n.,* mushroom. Also TALINGA q.v.

PAPAIT: *n.,* love spell worked through the agency of a charmed object which is hidden in the house or the possessions of the intended victim. When found the charmed object loses its power. Also sometimes used to mean sorcery where the charmed object is hidden in the same manner.

PAPA TRU: *n.,* biological father; SIMOL PAPA- uncle.

PAREI: *n.,* and *v.i.,* cheer.

PAS: *a.,* tight, fastened, tied, firm; *adv.,* ahead, forward; *n.,* letter, note, pass.

PASENSA MERI: *n.,* travelling prostitute.

PASIM: *v.t.,* tie, bind, block progress or advance, close, shut, capture, fasten, prevent, stop.

PASIN: *n.,* habit, way, custom, manner.

PASIS: *n.,* bay, inlet, passage, corridor, laneway.

PASKA: Easter.

PASLAIN: *n.,* forepart of a line or file, position in advance of general body. PASLAIN LONG... – before ...

PASPAS: *n.,* armlet or anklet of woven grass, basket-work on weapons or tools.

PASTAIM: *adv.,* once, before, first, first of all; for a while.

PATER: *n.,* priest, father.

PATI: *n.,* political party.

PAT. PATPELA: *a.,* fat.

PATO: *n.,* duck.

PATOGUS: *n.,* goose.

PATRIAK: *n.,* patriarch.

PATRON: *n.,* dynamite.

PAUDA: *n.,* fireworks, gunpowder.

PAUL: *n.,* fowl or hen; *v.i.,* tangle. PAULNABAUT- tangled.

PAUL BILONG BUS: *n.,* scrub turkey, scrub hen or bush fowl. Also WAIL PAUL.
PAULIM: *v.t.,* befoul, soil.
PAUS: *n.,* suitcase, portmanteau, purse, pouch.
PE: *n.,* wages, pay.
PEIM: *v.t.,* sell.
PEKATO: *n.,* sin.
PEKPEK: *n.,* faeces; *v.i.,* defaecate. HAUS PEKPEK- toilet.
PEN: *n.,* and *v.i.,* ache, pain; paint, ochre.
PENTEKOS: Pentecost.
PEPA: *n.,* pepper; paper, document.
PES: *n.,* forehead, page. Does not mean face.
PIK: *n.,* pig, pick, pickaxe, mattock.
PIKININI: *n.,* child, offspring, berry, nut or fruit of tree, seed.
PIKSA: *n.,* photograph, picture; *v.i.,* take a photograph.
PIKUS: *n.,* large tree, family *ficus*.
PILIM: *v.t.,* feel consequences of negligence, wrong doing, etc., feel tactually.
PILIM NOGUT: *v.i.,* not feel well, be in pain.
PILIM SKIN: *v.i.,* be decrepit, have stiffness of old age, be growing old; feel pain.
PILO: :*n.,* pillow.
PIN: *n.,* buckle, trouser buckle.
PINAS: *n.,* motor launch.
PINDUA: *n.,* window.
PINGA: *n.,* finger, toe.
PINIS: *a.,* finished; *adv.,* entirely, completely; also used with verbs to form the Past Participle – KAIKAI PINIS.
PINIS TAIM: *v.i.,* complete a contract of service or enlistment.
PIPI: *n.,* turkey.
PIPIA: *n.,* rubbish, refuse, discarded fragment; *a.,* useless.
PIPIA KLOS: *n.,* soiled linen, clothes, etc., for the laundry.
PIS: *n.,* fish.
PISIN: *n.,* general term for birds.
PISLAIN: *n.,* fishing line.
PISLAMA: *n.,* beche-de-mer or trepang.
PISPIS: *n.,* urine; *v.i.,* urinate.
PIT: *n.,* variety of wild sugar – family *graminaceae*. It is cultivated by the natives and the immature flower tassel cooked and eaten (probably *saccharum arundinaceum*). Often referred to as PITPIT.
PITPIT: *n.,* a variety of wild sugar growing in swamps and along watercourses *(saccharum spontaneum)*.

PIUS: *n.*, paper fuse of shillings amounting to five pounds; dynamite fuse.
PLAG: *n.*, ensign, flag.
PLAIAS: *n.*, pincers, pliers. See SANGGE.
PLANGK: *n.*, pine tree, war shield, plank, board.
PLANTI: *a.*, and *n.*, many, much, a lot, considerable number.
PLANTIM: *v.t.*, bury, set in the ground.
PLASTA: *n.*, surgical adhesive plaster.
PLAUA: *n.*, flour, flower. See PULPUL. Also wheatmeal.
PLE: *n.*, game, joke, gambol; *v.t.*, and *i.*, play, taking part in a game, joke, chaff; *a.*, jocular, bantering. Also means to have sexual intercourse. See Chapter VIII, p.28.
PLE KUK: *v.i.*, play a game of cards known as KUK.
PLE LAKI: *v.i.*, gamble at cards.
PLE NOGUT: *v.i.*, commit adultery, fornicate.
PLES: *n.*, village, one's homeland, region, district.
PLES BALUS: *n.*, aerodrome, landing ground.
PLES DAUN: *n.*, low lying ground; the Earth.
PLES KANAKA: *n.*, region lived in or owned by kanakas.
PLES NOGUT: *n.*, very rough stretch of ground, place of ill-omen.
PLES PLE: *n.*, playground.
PLET: *n.*, bowl, dish, plate.
PLET BOI: *n.*, native's feeding bowl issued on execution of a contract of service.
PLET KAIKAI: *n.*, dinner plate.
PLET MUSIK: *n.*, gramophone record.
PLET SUP: *n.*, soup plate.
PLOA: *n.*, floor.
POA: *num.*, four.
POAPELA: *num. a.*, four.
POBAITU: *n.*, rifle cleaning flannel.
POIN: *n.*, cape, promontory, mountain spur, river bend.
POISIN: *n.*, sorcery, evil spell, a sorcerer.
POK: *n.*, fork. See GABEL.
POLAIN: *v.i.*, form a line, fall in.
POLIS: *n.*, metal polish.
POLIS BOI: *n.*, native constable.
POLISIM: *v.t.*, polish, shine.
POLISMASTA: *n.*, police officer in the European Police; cadet in the District Services.
POMUT: *n.*, potassium permanganate.
PONDE: *n.*, Thursday.
POPAIA: *v.i.*, (of a missile) to miss the target or object aimed at.
POPI: *n.*, and *a.*, Catholic.

POPIS: *n.,* porpoise.
POPO: *n., (carica papaya)* pawpaw.
PORET: *n.,* forward, front, bow of ship; *adv.,* towards the front, in front.
POS: *n.,* post, upright pole.
POSAI: *n.,* and *a.,* albino.
POTO: *n.,* photograph.
PRAIM: *v.t.,* fry.
PRAIPAN: *n.,* frypan.
PRAM: *n.,* span of the arms from fingertip to fingertip; a fathom.
PRANIS: *n.,* primus stove.
PRAUWIN: *n.,* following wind.
PREN: *n.,* friend, term of address; *v.i.,* have extramarital intercourse or fornicate without payment but by consent; PREN LONG . . . (of a woman) offer herself to a man without payment.
PRENIS: *prop.a.,* and *n.,* Italian, French, France.
PRESEN: *n.,* gift; *v.i.,* give a present; (police) present arms.
PRET: *n.,* timid, cautious, afraid, apprehensive, chary; PRETIM- frighten.
PRISTA: *n.,* priest.
PROG: *n.,* leather or webbing bayonet frog. Frog is ROKROK.
PROKSAIT: *n.,* peroxide.
PROKWIN: *n.,* wooden dish or bowl made by the natives and somewhat like our meat dish, but deeper.
PROMAN: *n.,* mate, companion, one of a pair.
PRUT: *n.,* fruit, tinned fruit, peach, peach tree, large coastal tree producing edible fruits.
PUINGA: *n.,* fart. Also KAPOPO.
PUKPUK: *n.,* crocodile; person affected with GRILE (q.v.).
PUL: *n.,* canoe paddle, oar; *v.i.,* row, paddle.
PULAP: *a.,* full.
PULAPIM: *v.t.,* fill with – PULAPIM WARA LONG BAKET.
PULBOT: *n.,* rowboat, dinghy.
PULIM: *v.t.,* paddle a canoe, row a boat, draw a pull-through through a gun, lead a file of carriers, haul.
PULIM: *v.t.,* coax, persuade, inveigle, oblige; rape.
PULMAN: *n.,* fool, stupid person.
PULPUL: *n.,* flower, grass skirt, tassels.
PULSEN: *n.,* zip fastener.
PUNPUN: *n.,* tree of acacia family growing in stony soil, generally on open plains. Wood is tough and tree grows to height of about 9 metres with a sparse foliage of pinnate leaves. *(Albizzia* spp.) (commonest – *A. procera).*
PUNDAUN: *v.i.,* fall, fall down, drop.
PUNUPUK: *n.,* restoration to grace; most generally used to describe the

soul's change of status after baptism.
PURGATORIO: *n.*, Purgatory.
PUS: *n.*, sash, scarf, head ribbon.
PUSI: *n.*, cat; rabbit; WAILPUSI- bushcat.
PUSIM: *v.t.*, (with man as subject) copulate with.
PUSPUS: *n.*, copulation; *v.i.*, copulate.
PUTIM: *v.t.*, put (it) in or into, place, apply; cause to be imprisoned.

RABIS: *a.*, poor, impoverished, containing or possessing things of no value.
RABISMAN: *n.*, impoverished person, beggar, no-hoper.
RAI: *n.*, S.E. trade wind.
RAIFEL: *n.*, rifle.
RAIS: *n.*, rice.
RAIT: *v.i.*, write.
RAITHAN: *n.*, right hand side, right hand.
RAM: *n.*, rum.
RAPIM: *v.t.*, rub, scrape.
RARING: *v.i.*, pray.
RAT: *n.*, rat, mouse (LIKLIK RAT- mouse).
RAUN: *a.*, round, circular.
RAUNPELA: *a.*, round, circular.
RAUNWARA: *n.*, lake, lagoon.
RAUNIM: *v.t.*, surround, encompass, wrap round, bind round.
RAUNWIN: *n.*, whirlwind.
RAUS: *v.imp.*, go! clear out! out of the way!
RAUSIM: *v.t.*, empty, discharge from service, send away, throw away, clear away. Clear the table after a meal is TEKEWE.
REN: *n.*, rain; *v.i.*, rain – REN I KAM DAUN.
RERE: *a.*, prepared, ready, set for action.
REREIM: *v.t.*, prepare, make ready.
RESA: *n.*, razor. KAPA RESA- razor blade.
RESIS: *n.*, race, contest of speed; *v.i.*, race, compete.
RET: *a.*, red, brown, chestnut, pink; IM I RET- it's red.
RETPELA: *a.*, red brown, chestnut, pink – RETPELA LAPLAP.
RIDIMA: *n.*, Redeemer.
RIKIN: (Naut.) *n.*, shrouds.
RING: *n.*, finger ring, small ring, bangle, armlet.
RIP: *n.*, reef.
RIPSEL: *n.*, reefsail.
RIT: *v.i.*, to read. RITIM: *v.t.*, read. See also KAUNTIM.
RON: *v.i.*, run, move quickly.
RONEWE: *v.i.*, run away, desert, remove oneself from the occasion of trouble or embarrassment.

RON I GO: *v.i.,* progress by running or swift movement.
RONIM: *v.t.,* chase; also RONRONIM- persistent pursuit.
RONG: *n.,* offence, misconduct.
ROP: *n.,* rope, vine, rattan cane, vein, artery.
ROS: *n.,* corrosion, rust.
ROT: *n.,* track, road, path, course.
RUKSACK: *n.,* rucksack.
RUM: *n.,* room, cubicle, stall, cabin.
RURU: *v.i.,* meditate.

SAINA: *n.,* China, Chinese.
SAINAMAN: *n.,* Chinese.
SAIOR: *n.,* general term for edible leaves. Also KUMU.
SAITAN: *n.,* sergeant.
SAK: *n.,* shark. SAK ANGGAU- dogfish.
SAKET: *n.,* jacket.
SAKIM: *v.t.,* disregard (warning or advice), cause an object to quiver or shake. SAKIM TOK- disobey.
SAKMAN: *n.,* martinet, strict person; *a.,* severe, harsh.
SAKRAMENTO: *n.,* Sacrament.
SAKSAK: *n.,* sago palm – *metroxylon sagus*. From which our sago is obtained. Grown in swampy ground and the trunk contains a firm starchy pith which is beaten by the natives and washed free of fibre, thus producing cakes of starchy extract of metroxylon, also called saksak. This, when cooked, is a very good substitute for commercial sago. The fronds are used for thatch and are sometimes included in term MAROTA.
SALAMON: *n.,* ceremonial rattles.
SALIM: *v.t.,* send, dispatch, give.
SAMAN: *n.,* outrigger of a canoe.
SAMAP: *v.i.,* sew; *n.,* stitching; *v.t.,* SAMAPIM.
SAMBAI: *v.i.,* watch over, protect, guard, be ready, stand by.
SAMPEPA: *n.,* small tree with large scabrous leaf; sandpaper.
SAMTING: *n.,* an article, something, thing. Also is a polite term for the external genital organs.
SAMTING NATING: *n.,* thing of no consequence.
SAMTING TRU: *n.,* thing of consequence.
SAN: *n.,* sun, sunlight, daytime.
SANAP: *v.i.,* stand, stand up; *v.t.,* SANAPIM.
SANDE: *n.,* Sunday; *v.i.,* pool tobacco, spend Sunday. (See p.45.)
SANG: *n.,* hard straight-grained timber *(vitex cofasus)* with yellow sapwood.
SANGANA: *n.,* inner side of thigh.
SANGGE: *n.,* pincers (also KUKA).

SANGGUMA: *n.* The term originally comes from Madang where it was used to describe a species of malign sorcery and also the person gifted with the power of performing it. It was performed by bringing about an apparent mesmerism of the victim by the sorcerer who then led him to his assistants and then thorns were pushed into parts of the body where it was desired pain or illness would manifest itself and eventually cause the death of the victim. A short thorn was pushed into the tongue causing it to swell so that the victim could not talk and tell the name of the sorcerers. The thorns were dipped in a special secret brew which apparently rendered them poisonous. The victim invariably died. The term has spread to other parts of the Territory to describe similar sorcery where the victim first undergoes mesmerism or is frozen with fright.

SANGSANGANA: *n.*, twins.

SANTA: *n.*, bottled perfume.

SAP: *a.*, sharp.

SAPA: *n.*, adze.

SAPIM: *v.t.*, sharpen, carve, put a point on, trim.

SAPOS: *conj.*, if, on condition that, whether; SAPOS ... NO- unless. *Vide* grammar.

SARAP: *v.imp.*, be quiet! shut up!

SARAT: *n.*, stinging nettle – family *urticaceae*. Often used by the natives as a counter irritant.

SAREL: *n.*, saddle. SARELIM: *v.i.*, saddle.

SARIP: *n.*, grass knife: SARIPIM- to cut grass, mow.

SASAIT: *n.*, exercise, drill (police and Army).

SATADE: *n.*, Saturday.

SAUA: *n.*, soursop – *annona muricata*. A small tree about 3 to 9 metres high. Grows in the the tropics and has leathery, obovate to elliptical leaves, 7 to 15 cms long. The fruit is ovoid, heart-shaped, oblong-conical and deep green with numerous short fleshy spines on the surface. The flesh is white, juicy and cottony and is delicious.

SAVE: *v.t.*, know, be aware of, understand, be cognisant with, be accustomed to, be acquainted with; *interrog.* – understand.

SAVETOK: *n.*, interpreter.

SEKHAN: *n.*, peace, friendship; friend; *v.i.*, make peace, shake hands.

SEKI: *a.*, impertinent, insolent, pert.

SEL: *n.*, sail, tent fly, canvas awning. HAUS SEL- tent.

SELA: *n.*, sailor; *a.*, after the fashion of a sailor, a hard doer.

SELPAN: *n.*, groundsheet.

SELPIS: *n.*, sailfish, marlin.

SEKIM: *v.t.*, see SAKIM.

SEM: *n.,* embarrassment, contrition, shame, humility, loss of face.
SEMIM: *v.t.,* humiliate, cause embarrassment to, shame.
SEN: *n.,* chain.
SENIS: *v.i.,* change places.
SENISIM: *v.t.,* exchange, swap, change, replace.
SENTA: *n.,* bottled perfumes.
SERT: *n.,* shirt.
SETAN: *n.,* Satan.
SEV: *v.i.,* shave.
SEWA: *n.,* range target. SIUT SEWA- range firing.
SEWEN: *ord.* and *card. numeral,* seven.
SEWENDE: *n.,* Seventh-day Adventist Mission.
SEWENPELA: *num.a.,* seven.
SI: *n.,* sea swell, waves.
SIA: *n.,* chair, stool.
SIAM: *n.,* jam.
SIAMAN: *n.,* and *a.,* German.
SIBUM: *n.,* jib boom of sailing boat.
SIGAR: *n.,* cigar.
SIK: *a.,* ill; *n.,* epidemic, sickness; SIK BOLONG MUN- menstruation period; SIKMAN- a patient.
SIKAU: *n.,* bandicoot, wallaby, kangaroo rat.
SIKHAUS: *n.,* sanitary closet (i.e., "dunny"). Also SMOL HAUS.
SIKISPELA: *num.a.,* six.
SILIKA: *n.,* silk, silk headband; *a.,* silken.
SILING: *n.,* 10 cents, 10 toea.
SIMEN: *n.,* cement, cement post, boundary mark.
SINDAUN: *v.i.,* sit, sit down, squat. SINDAUN LONG- live at.
SINGAUT: *v.i.,* call, yell.
SINGAUTIM: *v.t.,* call.
SINGGLIS: *n.,* singlet, undershirt, jersey, T-shirt.
SINGSING: *n.,* song, ceremonial dancing and singing, party; *v.i.,* sing, take part in a singsing.
SIOT: *n.,* shirt.
SIP: *n.,* ship.
SIPRAM: *n.,* rock in the sea, just under the water and constituting a danger to shipping.
SIPSIP: *n.,* sheep.
SIS: *n.,* cheese.
SISIS: *n.,* scissors.
SISA: *n.,* sibling of opposite sex (can be either male or female). Often SUSA.
SITBET: *n.,* bed sheet.
SIT BILONG LAM: *n.,* lamp black.

SIT BILONG PAIA: *n.,* ashes, soot.
SITHAUS: *n.,* sanitary closet (i.e., "dunny"). Also SMOL HAUS.
SIU: *n.,* boot, shoe.
SIUBIM: *v.t.,* push, shove.
SIUT: *v.i.,* shoot, fire a rifle; *n.,* (naut.) dipping line, mainsheet.
SIUTBOI: *n.,* servant whose duty is to shoot game.
SIUTIM: *v.t.,* shoot, pierce, stab.
SIUTLAM: *n.,* electric torch, flashlight.
SIUTSEWA: *v.i.,* shoot on a range or at a musketry training target.
SKEL: *n.,* balance or spring scales; rations.
SKELIM: *v.t.,* weigh, measure out quantities, share out.
SKELMAN: *n.,* unmarried man.
SKIN: *n.,* skin, peel covering, sheath.
SKIN DIWAI: *n.,* bark.
SKIN TORASEL: *n.,* tortoise shell.
SKOL: *n.,* squall.
SKON: *n.,* scone, damper.
SKRAP: *v.i.,* scratch; itch.
SKRAPIM: *v.t.,* grate, cut into fine pieces, chop up; scratch, irritate.
SKRAPIM LO- break the law.
SKRAPIM BEL: make angry.
SKRU: *n.,* elbow, knee, joint.
SKRUDRAIWA: *n.,* screwdriver.
SKRU I LUS: *n.,* injured knee.
SKRUIM: *v.t.,* twist, turn, misrepresent, maliciously misreport, tergiversate.
SKRUIM WANTAIM- join.
SKUL: *n.,* school.
SKULANKA: *n.,* classes somewhere between opportunity and vocational.
SKULIM: *v.t.,* coach, train, school, direct someone in a conspiracy.
SKUNA: *n.,* masted motor boat, schooner, ketch, yawl.
SLAPIM: *v.t.,* slap.
SLEK: *n.,* looseness, play, slack; *a.,* loose, slack.
SLEKIM: *v.t.,* make slack, pay out (a line), loosen.
SLING: *n.,* sling, musket sling, braces.
SLIP: *v.i.,* sleep, be unconscious, lie prone or at full length, lie down.
SLIPIM: *v.t.,* lay lengthways.
SMEL: *n.,* odour, scent, smell; *v.i.,* have a bad smell. SMEL NO GUT- stink.
SMELIM: *v.t.,* smell, sniff.
SMOK: *n.,* cigarette, tobacco, smoke; *v.i.,* smoke, smoke tobacco.
SMOKIM: *v.t.,* smoke; cure or dry by smoking.
SMOL HAUS: *n.,* outside toilet. See SIKHAUS, SITHAUS.
SMOLMAMA: *n.,* aunt.
SMOLPAPA: *n.,* paternal uncle.

SMOLPELA: *a.,* little, small, diminutive.
SNEK: *n.,* snake, worm, leech.
SNEKNABAUT: *a.,* winding, tortuous.
SO: *n.,* saw.
SOA: *n.,* ulcer, sore; *a.,* sore, painful.
SOIM: *v.t.,* indicate, show (something); cut with a saw.
SOK: *n.,* blackboard chalk.
SOKEN: *n.,* sock, stocking.
SOL: *n.,* salt, shoulder.
SOLAP: *v.i.,* swell, bulge.
SOLDA: *n.,* solder.
SOLMARESIN: *a.,* managanese sulphate (Epsom Salts).
SOLWARA: *n.,* sea, ocean, saltwater.
SOP: *n.,* soap.
SOPIS: *n.,* sawfish.
SORI: *n.,* sorrow, sadness; gladness arising out of a memory or reminiscence; gratitude, remembrance; *a.,* sad, sorry for, feel for, think of with feeling, sorry; *adv.,* compassionately, with pity, sadly, condolingly; also exclamation meaning Good!; or expressing sympathy in relation to misfortune, or gladness in relation to good fortune; also a term of greeting meaning "Glad to see you!" Nostalgia.
SOSIS: *n.,* sausages, sausage, saveloy.
SOSPEN: *n.,* saucepan, pot.
SOTPELA: *a.,* short, thickset, nuggety, squat.
SOTWIN: *a.,* panting, out of breath; pant after; long for- SOTWIN LONG- .
SOVEL: *n.,* shovel, spade.
SPANA: *n.,* spanner.
SPED: *n.,* spade.
SPET: *n.,* spittle; *v.i.,* expectorate.
SPETIM: *v.t.,* spit on, put spittle on.
SPIA: *n.,* arrow, spear.
SPIK: *v.i.,* speak, say. TOK I SPIK- spoke and said.
SPIRIS: *n.,* methylated spirits.
SPUN: *n.,* spoon.
STA: *n.,* star.
STAP: *v.i.,* be, remain, rest, be in progress, be present.
STAP GUT: *v.i.,* be well, be in good order, behave oneself.
STAS: *n.,* starch.
STESIN: *n.,* town, barracks, police post, Administrative headquarters.
STIA: *n.,* rudder, steering paddle, handlebars of bicycle; *v.i.,* to steer.
STIABOT: *n.,* starboard or right side of a ship.
STIAMAN: *n.,* helmsman, pilot.
STIK: *n.,* stick, haft, twig.

STIL: *v.i.,* sneak, creep, stalk, steal, act covertly; *n.,* covert act.
STILIM: *v.t.,* take possession of wrongfully, steal or thieve, rape, violate, have intercourse with a woman without husband's or parents' consent.
STILMAN: *n.,* thief, sneak.
STIMA: *n.,* steamship.
STINGK: *v.i.,* stink; *a.,* rotted, decayed.
STINGRE: *n.,* stingray.
STIRAP: *n.,* bicycle pedal; stirrup.
STON: *n.,* stone, rock.
STORI: *n.,* tale, a history, account.
STOV: *n.,* stove.
STRAIP: *n.,* chevron.
STRET: *a.,* correct, right, true, straight.
STRETIM: *v.t.,* make straight, tidy, unravel, set right, correct, settle a difference or misunderstanding, level out.
STRING: *n.,* string.
STRONG: *a.,* determined, strong-willed; *adv.,* sturdily, with strength.
STRONGPELA: *a.,* sturdy, strong, robust, powerful.
STRONGPELA MARESIN: *n.,* acid.
STRONGPELA SOA: *n.,* tropical ulcer.
STUA: *n.,* shop, store, storehouse, pantry.
SUA: *n.,* shore; GO SUA- Disembark.
SUKA: *n.,* sugar, sugar cane.
SUMATIN: *n.,* schoolboy.
SUP: *n.,* soup.
SUPKAR: *n.,* wheelbarrow. See WILKA.
SUPSUP: *n.,* fish spear.
SURIK: *v.i.,* retire, go back, reverse; cower, flinch, start back.
SURIKIM: *v.t.,* ease back, work back, edge back.
SUSAP: *n.,* Jew's harp.
SUSU: *n.,* milk, breast, udder, tinned milk; also a deep, narrow fish of milky whiteness, about 38 cms long and found about reefs and belonging to the trevally family (milkfish).
SWIM: *v.i.,* to swim; *v.t.,* SWIMIM.
SWIT: *a.,* sweet, sugary.
SWITMULI: *n.,* orange.

TABAK: *n.,* Leprosy; stick tobacco.
TAIA: *n.,* tyre.
TAID: *n.,* current, torrent; *v.i.,* have a strong current.
TAIM: *n.,* time, period; *adv.,* when; HAUMAS TAIM?- how many times?
TAIM BIPO: *adv.,* before, once, previously.
TAIM NOGUT: *n.,* stormy weather, time of storms or other troubles.

TAIT: *a.,* firm, tight, taut; *adv.,* firmly.
TAITIM: *v.t.,* make firm, tighten, close up (line, formation), haul on, pull.
TAKIS: *n.,* tax; TROMWE TAKIS- pay tax.
TAKONDO: *a.,* holy, sanctified, blessed; *n.,* saint; DEWEL TAKONDO- Holy Spirit; TRINITAS TAKONDO- Holy Trinity.
TALAI: *n.,* sardines.
TALASA: *n.,* tall horizontally-branched tree with oblate leaves about 10 cms long and bearing a small thin-walled nut in a green skin.
TALATALA: *a.,* and *n.,* Protestant.
TALIBUNG: *n.,* green snail shell; *Turbo mamorata.*
TALINGA: *n.,* mushroom, edible fungus. Also PAPAI.
TALIS: *n., Terminalia Catappa,* durable elastic timber, edible nut (Indian chestnut).
TAMBARAN: *n.,* ghost, spirit; *a.,* ghostly.
TAMBILUA: *n.,* yaws, sores on sole of foot. See TONO.
TAMBU: *a.,* forbidden, sacred; *n.,* prohibition; relatives in-law whose name may not be mentioned; also a friendly term of address. Also very small shell - *nassavius* species - which is used as currency and decoration.
TAMBUN: *n.,* medium sized tree about 7.6 metres high *(Tripetalum cymosum, forma pendula).*
TAMIOK: *n.,* axe, hatchet, tomahawk.
TANG: *n.,* tongue.
TANGK: *n.,* water tank.
TANKET: *n.,* plant - *taetsia fruticosa* of family *liliaceae.* Grows 1 to 3 metres high, sparingly branched and leaves may be pink, purple, green, yellowish or white-spotted. Stem bears a cluster of spirally arranged leaves which are a long shiny oblong blade with a grooved stalk; branched, drooping flower cluster about 30 cms long and bearing numerous white, purple-tipped buds, and later red berries. Erroneously called *dracaena.* Also name given to those leaves worn in the back of the belt, in some parts of New Guinea, to cover the buttocks. These leaves are also much used in ceremony and to make a tambu on property, gardens, etc.
TANIM: *v.t.,* turn, twist, revolve, stir.
TANIM BEK: *v.t.,* turn over, turn about, bend back.
TANIM BEL: *v.t.,* change of mind.
TANIMTOK: *n.,* interpreter.
TANTANIM: *v.t.,* twist, twine, stir.
TAPEL: *n.,* slate.
TAPIOK: *n.,* tapioca plant and food *(Manihot Utilissima),* cassava.
TAPULIT: *n.,* tarpaulin.
TARANGAU: *n.,* hawk, eagle.

TARO: *n., (colocasia esculentium)* similar in appearance to the Calla Lily. Leaves are large and hastate in upright clusters with a grooved fleshy stem. It is a marsh plant and the roots act as storing organs for starch and so form the staple diet of many tribes. Term also includes the roots. It is cultivated and, in some areas, water is brought to the taro cultivations through many miles of bamboo pipeline. A variety known as Taro Kong Kong is not willingly cultivated. A lush leafed plant with a meagre tuber, it grows wild and is used in times of scarcity.

TARONGGU: *n.,* and *a.,* unfortunate; *a.,* unlucky.

TASOL: *conj.,* if, but; *adv.,* only, merely, nothing more; suppositive if or when; *a.,* sole, only. *Vide* p.25.

TAUKA: *n.,* cuttle fish.

TAUL: *n.,* conch shell horn made from *Triton tritonis;* towel.

TAUN: *n.,* large tree *(pomedia pinnata)*, medium hardwood of pink to light red brown colour with edible fruit.

TAUNEM: *n.,* mosquito net.

TAWAL: *n.,* black earthlike substance used to stain teeth black in initiation ceremony.

TEBAL: *n.,* table, shelf.

TEBAL TAMBU: *n.,* altar.

TEDE: *adv.,* today.

TEKEWE: *v.t.,* remove, clear away.

TEL: *n.,* tail.

TELAFON: *n.,* telephone.

TELIMAUTIM: *v.t.,* reveal, tell.

TEMATAN: *n.,* heathen.

TENKYU: Thank you!

TI: *n.,* brewed tea. Dry tea is LIP TI.

TIN: *n.,* can, tin container.

TINGK: *v.i.,* think, be of opinion; NO KEN TINGKIM- don't worry about (it), don't be embarrassed about (it).

TINGKIM: *v.t.,* think, estimate, consider.

TINGKTINGK: *n.,* thought, idea, opinion.

TIN KARASIN: *n.,* kerosene tin.

TIN MIT: *n.,* tin of meat.

TIN TALAI: *n.,* tin of sardines.

TINTE: *n.,* ink. More generally INGK.

TIPOT: *n.,* teapot.

TIS: *n.,* teeth; TIS I PEN- toothache. Is also used in the singular.

TISA: *n.,* teacher.

TOK: *n.,* rumour, news, word, message; *v.i.,* speak, talk. HARIM TOK: *imp.* - obey.

TOKBOI: *n.,* Pidgin-English.

TOK BOKIS: *n.,* metonymous term used to describe an object by applying to it the name of another object or condition to which it has a somewhat metaphoric similarity. Ex., a lavalava made by sewing two lengths of cloth together lengthwise is called TULIP- i.e., two leaves (or strips); *v.,* to use such a term. Also means double talk, argot. See p.78.

TOKGRIS: *n.,* and *v.i.,* chat, small talk.

TOK HAIT: *n.,* secret.

TOKIM: *v.t.,* inform, tell.

TOK INGLIS: *n.,* English speech; *v.i.,* talk in English.

TOK KUSKUS: *n.,* legend, myth, fairy tale; *v.i.,* narrate legends, myths, etc.

TOK NOGUTIM: *v.t.,* abuse.

TOK PISIN: *n.,* Pidgin-English; *v.i.,* speak in Pidgin-English.

TOK PLE: *n.,* and *v.i.,* chaff, banter.

TOK PLES: *v.i.,* talk in one's mother tongue; *n.,* mother tongue.

TOKSAVE: *n.,* instructions, explanation; *v.t.,* explain, interpret.

TOK SIAMAN: *n.,* German speech; *v.i.,* speak German.

TOKTOK: *n.,* talk, chatter, language; *v.i.,* talk, speak together.

TOK TRU: *v.i.,* speak the truth.

TOK WIN: *n.,* empty boasting, rant; *v.i.,* rant, wax magniloquent.

TOLAI: *n.,* Rabaul native.

TOLO: *n.,* N.W. trade wind and the season thereof.

TOMATA: *n.,* leprosy. See KEMPE.

TON: *n.,* large hardwood tree with large pinafid leaves.

TONO: *n.,* wart on the sole of the foot.

TIPOT: *n.,* teapot.

TORASEL: *n.,* turtle.

TORO: See TOLO.

TRABEL: *n.,* action pursued in court, or by the police for an offence against a female. Also less generally trouble over any offence. Also TRAWEL.

TRAIM: *v.t.,* test, try, attempt, taste.

TRAK: *n.,* truck.

TRAUSIS: *n.,* pants, trousers.

TRAUT: *v.i.,* vomit.

TRET: *n.,* cotton thread.

TRI: *num. card.* and *ord.,* three, third.

TRINDE: *n.,* Wednesday.

TRINITAS TAKONDO: *n.,* Holy Trinity.

TRIPELA: *num.a.,* three.

TRITAIM: *num. adv.,* thrice.

TROMWE: *v.t.,* throw, throw away, throw out, toss; TROMWE HAN-punch.

TRU: *a.,* true; *adv.,* truthfully, really. TRU ANTAP!- So help me God!

TU: *card.* and *ord. num.,* two, second; *adv.,* too, also.

TUDAK: *a.,* and *n.,* dark, night.

TUHAT: *n.,* perspiration.

TULAIT: *n.,* and *a.,* light, daylight, dawn.

TULIP: *n.,* see KAMANGORO. Also a lavalava or sheet made by sewing two strips of cloth lengthwise.

TULTUL: *n.,* Government native official and interpreter in a village.

TUMAS: *adv.,* greatly, very much, too much. Forms the superlative with adjectives and adverbs.

TUMATO: *n.,* tomato.

TUMBUNA: *n.,* ancestor, grandparent; *a.,* grand- (children).

TUMORA: *adv.,* tomorrow, day after. HAP TUMORA- day after tomorrow.

TUNA: *n.,* saltwater eel.

TUNDE: *n.,* Tuesday.

TUPELA: *num. a.,* two.

TUPTUP: *n.,* lid, cover, cork.

TUTAIM: *adv.,* twice.

TUWING: *n.,* biplane.

TWAIN: *n.,* string, twine.

ULA: *n.,* species of fish.

UMBEN: *n.,* woman's net bag, fish or pig net.

URITA: *n.,* octopus.

UTUN: *n., Barringtonia speciosa.* family *Myrtaceae;* large, dark green coastal tree, generously branched with large leaves. Flowers are large with five white pink-edged petals and numerous long pink-tipped anthers. Native of Australia and Pacific Islands.

VAVADAUN: *n.,* Sacrament of Benediction.

VAVARAI: *n.,* and *v.,* Sacrament of Confession.

VINIVEL: *n.,* Lent.

VIRUA: See BIRUA.

WAIA: *n.,* wire.

WAIL: often an adjectival prefix indicating not domesticated, uncultivated or being in a wild state.

WAILIS: *n.,* radio, wireless, rumour, message; *v.i.,* spread news, gossip.

WAIL MAN: *n.,* savage, unsophisticated native of the interior.

WAIL PAUL : *n.,* see PAUL BILONG BUS.

WAIL PIK: *n.,* wild pig.

WAIT: *adj.,* white.

WAITLIVA: *n.,* lung. Often WETLIVA.

WAITMAN: *n.,* white man.

WAITPELA: *a.*, white.
WAIT PUS: *n.*, Paramount Luluai.
WAITSAN: *n.*, sand.
WAITSKIN: *n.*, white man, white-skinned.
WAN: *card.* and *ord. num.*, one, first.
WANDE: *n.*, Monday.
WANKAIN: *a.*, similar, of same kind of species, variety of, sort of.
WANPELA: *num.a.*, one; *a.*, alone.
WANPIS: *n.*, "lone wolf", a "loner", sole man or beast in a situation.
WANTAIM: *num.adv.*, once; *conj.*, together with, as well as, together.
WANWING: *n.*, monoplane.
WARA: *n.*, water, fresh water, river.
WARI: *n.*, problems, conflict, uncertainty (Mi gat wari long ... Em i wari bilongen).
WAS: *v.i.*, be on guard duty, watch, be in charge (of something), do sentry duty, look out (for); *n.*, watch, period of duty on guard.
WASAMARA: *interrog.*, why? for what reason?
WASIM: *v.t.*, wash, baptise.
WASWAS: *n.*, bath, wash baptism: *v.i.*, bathe, wash.
WATPO: *interrog.*, why? for what reason?
WE: *adv.*, where? whence?; away.
WEL: *n.*, oil; *a.*, greasy, slippery.
WELIM: *v.t.*, oil, grease.
WESTAP: *adv.*, where? well, where is it? where is ...? what happens?
WET: *v.i.*, wait; also imperative, Wait!
WETIM: *v.t.*, wait for.
WETKOT: *n.*, arrested person waiting to be charged.
WETLIVA: *n.*, lung.
WIK: *n.*, week.
WILKA: *n.*, wheelbarrow. Also SUPKAR.
WILWIL: *n.*, bicycle.
WIN: *n.*, wind, air, gas, breath.
WINDUA: *n.*, window. Also PINDUA.
WINIM: *v.t.*, defeat, surpass, beat, excel; blow.
WINIS: *n.*, winch, crane.
WISIL: *n.*, and *v.i.*, whistle.
WISIS: *n.*, personal desires, likes, habit.
WISKI: *n.*, whisky, alcoholic spirits.
WOK: *n.*, cultivation, garden, duty, employment, work; *v.i.*, work, pursue a task or investigation; WOK LONG ...
WOKABAUT: *v.i.*, walk, travel on foot; *n.*, stroll.
WOKBOI: *n.*, native indentured labourer.
WOKBUS: *v.i.*, work in the bush, cut through the bush.

WOKIM: *v.t.,* make, fashion, create, prepare, build.
WOKNAIT: *v.i.,* work at night.
WOKSAVE LONG: *v.t.,* investigate (a thing), examine or probe.
WOKURAI: *v.i.,* hold a conference, debate, arbitrate.
WONEM: *a.interrog.,* and *rel.,* what; exclamation - what!: NAU WONEM- indeed, of course.
WUSTA: *n.,* oyster.

YAM: *n.,* yam. *Dioscorea* spp. fam. *convolvulaceae.*
YAMBO: *n.,* guava.
YANGPELA: *a.,* young, unmarried.
YAR: *n.,* casuarina tree.
YAU: *n.,* ear.
YELO: *a.,* yellow; MULI EM I YELO; YELOPELA MULI.
YESA: *adv.,* yes, right ho, certainly sir!
YESUS: *n.,* Jesus.
YET: *adv.,* yet, still; affix meaning - self or personally, also to emphasise a pronoun; MI YET MI MEKIM- I, myself, did it.
YIAR: *n.,* year.
YIS: *n.,* yeast.
YOT: *n.,* iodine.
YU: *pron.,* you - second person singular.
YUMI: *pron.,* we, us - first person dual and plural.
YUPELA: *pron.,* you - second person plural.

ENGLISH TO NEO-MELANESIAN

LIST OF ABBREVIATIONS

a., adjective
adv., adverb
conj., conjunction
dem., demonstrative
excl., exclamation
imp., imperative
interrog., interrogative
miss., mission
n., noun
Naut., Nautical
neg., negative

num., numeral
p., pronoun
pers. personal
poss., possessive
pr., pronoun
prep., preposition
pron., pronoun
prop., proper
v., verb
v.i., verb intransitive
v.t., verb transitive

If the word you require is not listed, look for a word with a similar meaning.

A, AN: *indef. art.*, wanpela.
ABANDON: *v.t.*, lusim.
ABDOMEN: *n.*, bel.
ABET: *v.t.*, halpim.
ABILITY: *n.*, have ability – save tumas.
ABJECT: *a.*, rabis.
ABLAZE: *a.*, paia, lait.
ABLE: *a.*, be able to – ken, save, inap long.
ABNORMAL: *a.*, narakain.
ABODE: *n.*, haus; *v.i.*, stap.
ABOLISH: *v.t.*, rausim, katim.
ABORIGINAL: *n.*, kanaka.
ABOUND: *v.i.*, i pulap.
ABOUT: *prep.*, long; *v.i.*, baut: PUT THE ... ABOUT- bautim; *adv.*, nabaut; *a.*, klostu.
ABOVE: *adv.*, antap; *prep.*, antap long ...
ABSCESS: *n.*, buk.
ABSCOND: *v.i.*, ronwe.
ABSENT: *a.*, no i stap; *v.t.*, no kamap.
ABSOLUTELY: *adv.*, olgeta.
ABSOLVE: *v.t.*, larim.
ABSURD: *a.*, kranki, longlong.
ABUNDANCE: *a.*, planti; colloq., "gras bilong leg!".
ABUSE: *v.t.*, toknogutim.

ABUT: *v.i.,* abut on – go arere long.
ACCEPT: *v.t.,* kisim.
ACCLAIM: *v.t.,* hamamas long; parei long ...
ACCOMPANY: *v.t.,* go wantaim long ...
ACCOST: *v.t.,* go kamap long (to another), kam kamap long (to self).
ACCOUNT: *n.,* tok.
ACCUSE: *v.t.,* kotim, kolim, siutim tok long ...
ACCUSTOM: *v.t.,* lainim pesin bilong; *a.,* save.
ACHE: *v.i.,* and *n.,* pen.
ACID: *n.,* strongpela marasin; *a.,* i pait.
ACQUAINT: *v.t.,* tokim; selim tok long ... – ACQUAINT SOMEONE.
ACQUIRE: *v.t.,* kisim.
ACRID: *a.,* be acrid – i pait.
ACROSS: *prep.,* across the river – long hapsait long wara; lie across the table – slip narawe long tebol.
ACTIVE: *a.,* strong.
ACTUAL: *a.,* tru.
ACUMEN: *n.,* save.
ADAGE: *n.,* lo.
ADAPT: *v.t.,* inapim, wokim bai inap long ...
ADD: *v.t.,* putim; A. TO – skruim long.
ADDER: *n.,* snek.
ADDRESS: *v.t.,* tokim, orovasio long ...
ADEQUATE: *a.,* inap.
ADHERE: *v.i.,* adhere to ... – pas long, bihainim (follow).
ADJACENT: *a.,* klostu.
ADJUST: *v.t.,* stretim.
ADMINISTRATION: *n.,* Gavman.
ADMINISTRATOR: *n.,* Namba wan Gavman.
ADMIRE: *v.t.,* laikim tumas, mangal (but with some envy).
ADMONISH: *v.t.,* krosim.
ADORE: *v.t.,* lotu long ..., lotuim.
ADORN: *v.t.,* bilasim.
ADORNMENT: *n.,* bilas.
ADRIFT: *a.,* and *adv.,* drip.
ADROIT: *a.,* be adroit – save tumas.
ADULT: *n.,* bikpela, draipela bun.
ADULTERY: *n.,* plei nogut, trabel long meri.
ADVANCE: *n.,* go in advance – go pas; *n.,* pas.
ADVENTIST, SEVEN-DAY: *n.,* Sewende.
ADVISE: *v.t.,* lainim, skulim.
ADZE: *n.,* sapa; (slang – "Kongkong").
AEROPLANE: *n.,* balus. JET PLANE – boing.

AFAR: *adv.,* longwe.
AFFIRMATIVE: yesa, yes.
AFFLUENT: *a.,* bikpela, gat planti moni.
AFLOAT: *a.,* to be afloat – drip.
AFRAID: *a.,* pret.
AFTER: *prep.,* bihain long ..., *adv.,* bihain.
AFTERNOON: *n.,* apinum.
AFTERWARD: *adv.,* bihain.
AGAIN: *adv.,* gen, wantaim moa.
AGED: *a.,* lapun, as melum melum.
AGENT: *n.,* kuskus.
AGO: *adv.,* bipo.
AGONY: *n.,* bikpela pen.
AGREE: *v.i.,* agree to – orait long.
AGREEABLE: *a.,* orait, gutpela.
AGRICULTURE DEPT. OF: *n.,* Didiman. Also OFFICER of same.
AHEAD: *adv.,* pas; GO AHEAD- gohet.
AID: *v.t.,* halpim.
AIM: *v.t.,* slingim; AIM AT ... – makim.
AIR: *n.,* win.
AIRFIELD: *n.,* ples balus.
AIRPLANE: see AEROPLANE.
ALAS!: sore!
ALBINO: *n.,* and *a.,* posai.
ALIGHT: *a.,* lait, paiya: *v.i.,* pundaun.
ALIKE: *adv.,* olosem, wankain.
ALIVE: *a.,* i stap yet.
ALL: *a., n.,* and *adv.,* olgeta.
ALLEY: *n.,* pasis.
ALLOCATE: *v.t.,* makim.
ALLOW: *v.t.,* orait long.
ALL RIGHT: *a.,* orait.
ALLURE: *v.t.,* grisim, pulim.
ALMOST: *adv.,* klosap.
ALONE: *a.,* and *adv.,* wanpela tasol. See WANPIS.
ALONG: *prep.,* long.
ALONGSIDE: *adv.,* klostu long, arere long.
ALOUD: *adv.,* bikmaus.
ALREADY: *adv.,* pinis.
ALSO: *adv.,* tu.
ALTAR: *n.,* tebol tambu. ALTAR BOY- kundar.
ALTER: *v.t.,* senis, wokim gen.
ALTHOUGH: *conj.,* tasol.

ALTOGETHER: *adv.,* olgeta.
ALWAYS: *adv.,* oltaim.
AM: see grammar, p.24.
AMERICA: *prop.n.,* Amerika – also AMERICAIN.
AMID: *prep.,* long namil long ...
AMONG: *prep.,* namil long.
AMPLE: *a.,* bikpela, bik, planti, inap.
AMPUTATE: *v.t.,* katim.
ANCESTOR: *n.,* tumbuna.
ANCHOR: *n.,* anka.
ANCIENT: *a.,* bilong bipo.
AND: *conj.,* na, wantaim, q.v.
ANGEL: *n.,* anggelo.
ANGER: *n.,* kros.
ANGRY: *a.,* belihat, kros. BE ANGRY WITH- krosim. MAKE ANGRY- skrapim bel.
ANIMAL- no generic term.
ANIMOSITY: *n.,* kros.
ANKLE: *n.,* skru. Knee and elbow is also skru – so watch it.
ANKLET: *n.,* paspas bilong lek.
ANOTHER: *n.,* and *a.,* narapela.
ANSWER: *n., v.t.,* and *v.i.,* bekim. ANSWER BACK- bekim tok.
ANT: *n.,* anis. The coconut ant is korakum.
ANTIC: *n.,* ple.
ANY: *a.,* sampela.
ANYTHING: *n.,* wanpela samting; *a* maski, bringim wanpela samting i orait – don't worry, it's O.K. to bring ANYTHING.
APOSTLE: *n.,* Apostel.
APPEAR: *v.i.,* kamap.
APPOINT: *v.t.,* makim, putim.
APPORTION: *v.t.,* skelim, dilim, inapim.
APPROACH: *v.t.,* go (kam) klostu long ... go (kam) kamap.
APPROPRIATE: *a.,* inap, stret.
APPROVE: *v.t.,* orait long ...
APRIL: *n.,* April.
ARDENT: *a.,* hatpela.
ARE: see grammar p.24.
AREA (geog.): *n.,* hap.
ARGOT: *n.,* tok bokis.
ARID: *A.,* drai tru.
ARISE: *v.t.,* gerap.
ARM: *n.,* han.
ARMY: *n.,* ami.

ARMLET: *n.,* paspas, ring.
AROMA: *n.,* smel.
AROUND: *prep.,* put it around – raunim; go around – arova long ..., abirisim, raunim ...; *adv.,* nabaut.
AROUSE: *v.t.,* gerapim.
ARREST: *v.t.,* holimpas, pasim.
ARRIVE: *v.i.,* go (kam) kamap.
ARROGANT: *a.,* bikhet.
ARROW: *n.,* spia.
ARTICLE: *n.,* samting.
AS: *adv.,* olsem.
ASCEND: *v.t.,* goapim.
ASHAMED: *a.,* sem, malari.
ASHES: *n.,* sit bilong paia.
ASK: *v.t.,* or *i.,* askim.
ASKEW: *a.,* kronggut, no stret.
ASLEEP: *a.,* i slip, dai long slip.
ASPIRIN: *n.,* asprin.
ASSAULT: *v.t.,* paitim.
ASSENT: *v.i.,* ASSENT TO- orait long ..., yes long ...
ASSIGN: *v.t.,* makim.
ASSIST: *v.t.,* alivim, halpim.
ASSISTANT DISTRICT OFFICER: *prop.n.,* namba tu kiap.
ASTERN, GO: *v.i.,* surik, gostan.
ASTONISHED, BE: *v.i.,* gerap nogut.
AT: *prep.,* long.
ATE: *v.t.,* kaikai pinis, kaikaim.
ATONE: *v.i.,* bekim.
ATTACH: *v.t.,* pasim.
ATTACK: *v.t.,* go pait long, kalap long, bungim.
ATTEMPT: *v.t.,* traim, laik ...
ATTIRE: *n.,* klos; ATTIRED IN A LAPLAP- pasim laplap.
ATTRACT: *v.t.,* pulim.
AUGER: *n.,* boa.
AUGUST: *n.,* Augus.
AUNT: *n.,* mama, smolmama.
AUTHORITY: *n.,* nem, namba.
AVENGE: *v.t.,* bekim.
AVERT: *v.t.,* sakim.
AVOCADO: *n.,* bata, (*Persea* sp.)
AVOID: *v.t.,* abrusim, ronwe long ...
AWAIT: *v.t.,* wetim, wet long.
AWAKE: *v.i.,* gerap; *a.,* i no slip.

AWAKEN: *v.t.,* gerapim.
AWARE: *a.,* be aware – save.
AWE: *n.,* pret.
AWKWARD: *a.,* hewe, kranki.
AWRY: *a.,* kronggut.
AXE: *n.,* akis, tamiok.

BABY: *n.,* pikinini.
BACK: *n.,* baksait, bihain; *adv.,* bek; *v.i.,* surik, gostan. BACK AND FORTH- i go i kam.
BAD: *a.,* nogut.
BADGE: *n.,* mak, namba.
BAG: *n.,* bek; STRING BAG- bilum, KITBAG- kikbek.
BAGGAGE: *n.,* kago.
BAIL: *v.t.,* biloim (canoe).
BAILER: *n.,* bilo (q.v.).
BAILER SHELL: *n.,* gam.
BAIT (fish): *n.,* kaikai bilong huk.
BAKE: *v.t.,* kukim long aven.
BAKERY: *n.,* haus bret.
BALANCE: *v.i.,* and *t.,* skel, skelim.
BALCONY: *n.,* beranda.
BALD: *a.,* kela.
BALL: *n.,* bal.
BAMBOO: *n.,* mambu. See also kaul.
BANANA: *n.,* banana; WILD BANANA- karapua.
BANDAGE: *n.,* banis.
BANDICOOT: *n.,* mumut.
BANG: *v.t.,* bengim.
BANGLE: *n.,* ring.
BANISH: *v.t.,* rausim.
BANK: *n.,* haus moni; RIVER BANK- sua, arere bilong wara.
BANQUET: *n.,* kaikai; GIVE A BANQUET- mekim kaikai.
BANTER: *v.t.,* tok plei long ...; *n.,* tokplei.
BAPTISM: *n.,* Baptismo, Waswas; *v.t.,* baptaisim.
BAR: *v.t.,* pasim, banisim, tambuim.
BARBARIAN: *n.,* buskanaka, manambus.
BARK: *n.,* skin diwai; BARK OF A DOG- krai bilong dok; *v.i.,* dok i krai.
BARRACUDA: *n.,* malisa.
BARREL: *n.,* kas.
BARRICADE: *n.,* banis.
BARROW: *n.,* wilka, supkar.
BARTER: *v.t.,* peim.

BASE: *n.*, as.
BASHFUL: *a.*, sem.
BASIN: *n.*, plet, dis.
BASKET: *n.*, basket.
BASTARD: *n.*, basat.
BAT: *n.*, liklik blakbokis; bat (cricket).
BATH: *n.*, waswas.
BATHE: *v.i.*, waswas.
BATTERY: *n.*, batari; CHARGE A B.- hotim batari.
BATTLE: *n.*, pait.
BAUBLE: *n.*, samting nating.
BAY: *n.*, pasis.
BAYONET: *n.*, benit.
BE: see grammar p.24. LET IT BE- larim i stap.
BEACH: *n.*, nambis, wetsan.
BEAD: *n.*, bis; ROSARY BEADS- kurkurua.
BEAK: *n.*, maus.
BEAN: *n.*, bin. WING BEAN- hasbin.
BEAR: *v.t.*, kakarim (birth): karim.
BEARD: *n.*, gras bilong maus. A BEARDED MAN is maus-gras.
BEAT: *v.t.*, paitim, hamarim; winim (defeat).
BEAUTIFUL: *a.*, naispela, nais.
BECAUSE: *conj.*, bilong.
BED: *n.*, bet.
BEDECK: *v.t.*, bilasim.
BEDROOM: *n.*, rum slip.
BEE: *n.*, ninik, binen.
BEEF: *n.*, abus, mit, bulmakau.
BEEN: *v.i.*, bin. (See TENSES p.24.)
BEER: *n.*, bia.
BEES' WAX: *n.*, meme bilong binatang; polis (floor polish).
BEETLE: *n.*, binatang.
BEFORE: *adv.*, bipo; *prep.*, bipo long ... (go) paslain long.
BEGGAR: *n.*, rabisman.
BEGIN: *v.i.*, kamap, gerap; *v.t.*, gerapim, bringim.
BEGUILE: *v.t.*, giamanim, grisim.
BEHAVE (oneself): *v.i.*, sindaun gut, stap gut.
BELIEVE: *v.t.*, tingim tru, bilipim.
BELL: *n.*, belo.
BELLY: *n.*, bel.
BELONG: *v.i.*, bilong.
BELOW: *adv.*, ananit, daunbilo; *prep.*, ananit long ...
BELT: *n.*, let; *v.t.*, hamarim, paitim.

BENCH: *n.,* bet, bank.
BEND: *v.t.,* krunggutim.
BENEATH: *adv.,* ananit; *prep.,* ananit long ...
BENEDICTION: *n.,* Vavadaun.
BENEVOLENT: *a.,* gutpela.
BENT: *a.,* krunggut.
BENZINE: *n.,* bensin.
BERRY: *n.,* pikinini bilong diwai, etc.
BESIDE: *prep.,* klostu long ...
BESIDES: *adv.,* na ...... tu.
BEST: *a.,* gutpela tumas, winim ol, namba wan. In the sense of the BEST THING TO DO- moa beta ...
BETEL NUT: *n.,* bilinat, buai. B. PEPPER- daka. WILD B.- kawiwi.
BETTER: *a.,* gutpela moa, moa gut; *adv.,* moa beta.
BETWEEN: *prep.,* namil long ...
BEWARE OF: *v.i.,* lukaut long.
BEWITCH: *v.t.,* wokim poisin (malira, papait) long ...
BIBLE: *n.,* Buk Tambu.
BICYCLE: *n.,* wilwil.
BIG: *a.,* bikpela.
BILLOW: *n.,* si.
BIND: *v.t.,* pasim.
BIPLANE: *n.,* tuwing.
BIRD: *n.,* pisin.
BIRD OF PARADISE: *n.,* kumul.
BISCUIT: *n.,* biskit.
BISHOP: *n.,* bisop.
BITCH: *n.,* dok meri.
BITE: *v.t.,* kaikai.
BITTER: *a.,* save pait.
BLACK: *a.,* blak, blakpela.
BLANKET: *n.,* blangket.
BLAZE: *v.i.,* and *n.,* paia.
BLEED: *v.i.,* blut i kapset.
BLEND: *v.t.,* tanim wantaim, abusim.
BLESS: *v.t.,* blesim, santuim.
BLIND: *a.,* ai pas; BLIND IN ONE EYE- matakiau.
BLOCK: *n.,* (pulley block) blok; *v.t.,* (boxing) blokim. See BAR.
BLOOD: *n.,* blut.
BLOOD VESSEL: *n.,* rop.
BLOT: *n.,* mak.
BLOUSE: *n.,* klos.
BLOW: *v.t.,* winim; *n.,* slap.

BLUE: *a.,* blu, blupela; *n.,* (washing blue) blu.
BLUFF: *n.,* giaman; *v.t.,* giamanim.
BLUNT: *a.,* no sap.
BOAR: *n.,* pik man.
BOARD: *n.,* plank (a ship); *v.t.,* goap long sip (bot).
BOAST: *v.i.,* tok bilas, bikmaus, tok win.
BOASTER: *n.,* bikmaus.
BOAT: *n.,* bot, sip.
BODY: *n.,* skin.
BOG: *n.,* ples melum melum.
BOIL: *n.,* buk; *v.t.,* boilim; *v.i.,* boil.
BOLT: *v.t.,* pasim, lokim; *n.,* skru, bol.
BONE: *n.,* bun.
BOOK: *n.,* buk.
BOOKKEEPER: *n.,* kuskus.
BOOM (Naut.): *n.,* bum.
BOOT: *n.,* siu.
BORDER: *n.,* arere.
BORE: *v.t.,* (a hole) borim; *n.,* boa.
BORROW: *v.t.,* kisim pastaim.m
BOSS: *n.,* bosboi, bos.
BOTANIST: *n.,* didiman.
BOTH: *a.,* tupela.
BOTTLE: *n.,* botol.
BOTTOM: *n.,* as, daunbilo.
BOUGH: *n.,* han (bilong diwai).
BOUGHT: *v.t.,* baiim pinis.
BOULDER: *n.,* ston.
BOUND: *v.i.,* kalap; *a.,* go arere long ... (bound by); *v.t.,* pasim.
BOUNDARY: *n.,* arere.
BOW: *n.,* (archer) banara; (Naut.) poret; *v.i.,* lindaun, baut.
BOWELS: *n.,* bel.
BOWL: *n.,* plet.
BOX: *n.,* bokis, kes; *v.i.,* boksin (boxing, sparring).
BOY: *n.,* manki.
BRACE: *v.t.,* pasim, taitim. BRACE AND BIT- boa.
BRACELET: *n.,* ring. WOVEN B.- paspas.
BRAG: *v.i.,* tok bilas.
BRAIN: *n.,* kru.
BRANCH: *n.,* han (h. diwai, h. bilong wara).
BRAND: *n.,* mak.
BRASS: *n.,* bras; BRASS BUTTONS, etc., – bras.
BRASSIERE: *n.,* banis susu.

BRAVE: *a.*, ... i no save pret.
BRAWL: *n.*, and *v.i.*, pait.
BREAD: *n.*, bret.
BREADFRUIT: *n.*, kapiak.
BREAK: *v.t.*, brukim, bagarapim.
BREAKFAST: *n.*, kaikai bilong moningtaim.
BREASTS: *n.*, susu.
BREATH: *n.*, win; BREATHE- pulim win.
BREATHLESS: *a.*, sotwin.
BREEZE: *n.*, kolwin (from the sea); paiawin (from the shore).
BRIBE: *v.t.*, baiim.
BRIDGE: *n.*, bris.
BRIDLE: *n.*, braidel.
BRIEF: *a.*, liklik.
BRIGHT: *a.*, lait.
BRILLIANT: *a.*, lait strong (or gutpela).
BRIM: *n.*, maus, arere.
BRING: *v.t.*, bringim, karim.
BRINK: *n.*, arere.
BRITAIN: *prop.n.*, Englan.
BRITISH: *n.*, Engglis.
BROAD: *a.*, bikpela, sotpela, braitpela. (Sotpela is relative to longpela for its meaning of "broad".)
BROADCAST: *v.i.*, and *tr.*, brotkas, brotkasim.
BROADEN: *v.t.*, opim moa.
BROKEN: *a.*, bruk.
BRONZE: *n.*, and *a.*, bras.
BROOM: *n.*, brum; *v.t.*, brumim.
BROTHEL: *n.*, haus pamuk.
BROTHER: *n.*, of a male – brata; of a female – sisa. See p.39. Of a religious order – bruda.
BROUGHT: *v.t.*, bringim, bringim pinis.
BROWN: *a.*, red, redpela.
BRUSH: *n.*, bros; *v.t.*, brosim.
BUCKLE: *n.*, pin.
BUFFALO: *n.*, karabu.
BUG: *n.*, ngos ngos.
BUGLE: *n.*, biugel.
BUILD: *v.t.*, wokim.
BULGE: *v.i.*, solap; *n.*, buk, bel.
BULKSTORE: *n.*, bakstua.
BULL: *n.*, bulmakau man.
BULLET: *n.*, bol.

BULLOCK: *n.*, bulmakau.
BULLSEYE: *n.*, bosai.
BUMP: *v.t.*, bengim.
BUNDLE: *n.*, mekpas.
BUNG: *n.*, ai.
BURN: *v.t.*, kukim, boinim; *v.i.*, paia.
BURST: *v.i.*, bruk, pairap.
BURY: *v.t.*, planim.
BUSH: *n.*, bus; JUNGLE- bikbus.
BUSHFOWL: *n.*, faul bilong bus, wail fowl.
BUSHRAT: *n.*, sikau.
BUSINESS: *n.*, wok, bisnis.
BUSY: *a.*, gat wok.
BUT: *conj.*, tasol.
BUTTER: *n.*, bata.
BUTTERFLY: *n.*, bembe.
BUTTOCK: *n.*, as.
BUTTON: *n.*, baten; *v.t.*, pasim.
BUY: *v.t.*, baiim.
BY: *adv.*, long; *prep.*, klostu long ...
BY-AND-BY: *adv.*, liklik taim.

CABBAGE: *n.*, kabis, seior.
CABIN: *n.*, (ship) rum.
CAGE: *n.*, kes.
CAJOLE: *v.t.*, grisim.
CAKE: *n.*, kek, kuken.
CALF: *n.*, pikinini bilong bulmakau, baksait bilong lek.
CALICO: *n.*, laplap.
CALL: *v.t.*, singautim; *n.*, krai, singaut.
CALLOPHYLLUM: *n.*, kalapilim, irotu.
CALM: *a.*, (sea) klin.
CAMERA: *n.*, bokis piksa.
CAN: *v.i.*, ken; *n.*, tin.
CANAL: *n.*, parut.
CANDLE: *n.*, kandel.
CANE: *n.*, kanda.
CANNOT: *v.i.*, no ken.
CANOE: *n.*, kanu. MON is a high-prowed canoe without an outrigger.
CANVAS: *n.*, kandis, sel.
CAP: *n.*, hat.
CAPE: *n.*, (geog.) poin; RAIN CAPE- kot rein.
CAPER: *n.*, ple; *v.i.*, kalap nabaut.

CAPRICE: *n.,* wisis.
CAPSIZE: *v.t.,* and *v.i.,* kapsaitim, kapsait.
CAPSICUM: *n.,* sotpela lombo.
CAPTAIN: *n.,* kepten.
CAPTIVE: *n.,* kalabus.
CAPTURE: *v.t.,* pasim, holimpas.
CAR: *n.,* motoka.
CARBUNCLE: *n.,* buk.
CARDS: (to play) – ple kas; *n.,* kat.
CARE: *v.t.,* take care of – lukaut long ..., lukautim. DON'T CARE- maski.
CAREFUL, BE: wos gut, lukaut.
CARELESS, BE: no tingim wok.
CARGO: *n.,* kago.
CARNAL KNOWLEDGE, HAVE: pusim, pakim, ple long ...
CARPENTER: *n.,* kamda.
CARRIER: *n.,* kagoboi.
CARRY: *v.t.,* karim.
CARTRIDGE: *n.,* katris.
CARVE: *v.t.,* sapim. C. a joint – katim.
CASE: *n.,* kes.
CASH: *n.,* moni.
CASHIER: *n.,* kuskus.
CASING: *n.,* skin.
CASK: *n.,* kas.
CASSAVA: *n.,* tapiok *(Manihot Utilissima).*
CASOWARY: *n.,* muruk.
CASTOR OIL: *n.,* kasawel.
CASUARINA: *n.,* yar *(Casuarineae sp.,* probably *equisetifolia).*
CAT: *n.,* pusi.
CATCH: *v.t.,* pasim, hukim, kisim.
CATFISH: *n.,* mausgras.
CATHOLIC: *n.,* Katolik, Popi.
CATTLE: *n.,* bulmakau.
CAUSE: *n.,* as; *v.t.;* mekim.
CAUTIOUS: *a.,* pret.
CAVE: *n.,* hul.
CEASE: *v.i.,* pinis, dai.
CEMENT: *n.,* simen.
CEMETERY: *n.,* matmat.
CENSURE: *v.t.,* krosim.
CENTRE: *n.,* namil.
CEREMONY: *a.,* singsing.
CHAIN: *n.,* sen; *v.t.,* pasim long sen.

122

CHAIR: *n.,* sia.
CHALK: *n.,* kampang, kraide.
CHANGE: *v.t.,* senisim; *v.i.,* senis.
CHANT: *n.,* and *v.i.,* singsing.
CHAPEL: *n.,* haus lotu.
CHARCOAL: *n.,* blakpela sit bilong paia.
CHARM: *n.,* papait, malira.
CHARY: *n.,* pret.
CHASE: *v.t.,* ronronim, ronim.
CHAT: *v.i.,* gris.
CHEAT: *v.t.,* giamanim.
CHECK: *v.t.,* pasim; makim.
CHEEK: *v.t.,* tok bilas long; *a.,* seki; *n.,* hapsait long maus.
CHEER: *n.,* and *v.i.,* parei.
CHEESE: *n.,* sis.
CHEST: *n.,* bros (anat.), bokis (box).
CHEW: *v.t.,* kaikai (long tis, i no daunim).
CHIEF: *a.,* namba wan; *n.,* luluai, kukurai, namba wan bos.
CHILD: *n.,* pikinini.
CHILLI: *n.,* lombo.
CHIMNEY: *n.,* paip (bilong stov).
CHIN: *n.,* wasket. In some areas- asket.
CHINA: *prop.n.,* Saina. CHINAMAN- Saina, Sainaman.
CHISEL: *n.,* maisel; cold chisel- kol sisel.
CHOICE: *n.,* laik.
CHOKE: *v.t.,* pasim win bilong .....
CHOOSE: *v.t.,* makim, laikim.
CHOP: *v.t.,* katim, katim liklik.
CHRISTMAS: *n.,* Krismas.
CHUCKLE: *v.i.,* lap.
CHUM: *n.,* poreman, pren.
CHURCH: *n.,* haus lotu.
CIGAR: *n.,* siga, brus.
CIGARETTE: *n.,* smok, sigaret.
CINEMA: *n.,* haus piksa.
CIRCLE: *n.,* ring.
CIRCULATE: *v.i.,* raunraun.
CITRON: *n.,* muli.
CLAM: *n.,* gamsel.
CLAMOUR: *v.i.,* bikmaus.
CLAN: *n.,* lain, bisnis, mismis, pisin. Latter is most used.
CLASS: *n.,* wankain, kain.
CLAW: *n.,* kapa, nil.

CLAY: *n.*, strongpela graun.
CLEAN: *a.*, klin; *v.t.*, klinim.
CLEAR: *a.*, klia; *v.t.*, kliarim, rausim; *v.i.*, raus. C. THE TABLE- tekewe.
CLEMENCY: *n.*, marmari.
CLERK: *n.*, kuskus.
CLEVER, BE: save tumas.
CLIMB: *v.t.*, goapim; *v.i.*, goap.
CLOCK: *n.*, klok.
CLOSE: *v.t.*, pasim; *adv.*, klostu. CLOSED: *a.*, pas.
CLOTH: *n.*, laplap.
CLOTHES: *n.*, klos. DINNER SUIT and the like – klos singsing.
CLOUD: *n.*, klaut, smok.
CLUSTER: *v.i.*, bung.
COAL TAR: *n.*, kol ta.
COAST: *n.*, nambis.
COAT: *n.*, saket.
COCKATOO: *n.*, koki.
COCKROACH: *n.*, kokoros.
COCOA: *n.*, koko.
COCONUT: *n.*, kokanas. See BILO, BOMBOM, BUN, DRAI, DRIP, GALIMBONG, KOPRA, KRU, KULAU, NOK.
COD: *n.*, (fish) bikmaus.
COERCE: *v.t.*, pulim.
COFFEE: *n.*, kopi.
COFFIN: *n.*, bokis.
COIL: *v.t.*, lotim, raunim, latapim.
COIN: *n.*, moni.
COLD: *a.*, kol.
COLLARDS: *n.*, kumu, saior.
COLLECT: *v.i.*, bung; *v.t.*, kisim na bungim- COLLECT TOGETHER.
COMB: *n.*, kom; *v.t.*, komim.
COMBAT: *n.*, pait.
COME: *v.i.*, kam, kamkamap.
COMPANION: *n.*, pren, proman.
COMPEL: *v.t.*, pulim.
COMPETE: *v.i.*, resis.
COMPLAIN: *v.i.*, kot.
COMPLETE: *v.t.*, pinisim.
COMPLETELY: *adv.*, olgeta.
COMPLICATED: *a.*, faulnabaut (of account, talk, etc.).
COMRADE: *n.*, proman.
CONCEIT: *n.*, bilas, bighet.
CONCERN: *n.*, wok.

CONCH HORN: *n.*, taul.
CONCLUDE: *v.t.*, pinisim; *v.i.*, pinis.
CONDUCT: *a.*, pesin. In the sense of TO LEAD- bringim.
CONFER: *v.i.*, wokurai, i.e., have a conference.
CONFERENCE: *n.*, kiwung.
CONFESS: *v.t.*, nukpuku long.
CONFESSION: *n.*, Varvarai.
CONFUSE: *v.t.*, mekim longlong; BE CONFUSED- longlong.
CONNECT: *v.t.*, pasim wantaim, skruim long.
CONQUER: *v.t.*, winim.
CONSENT: *v.i.*, orait (long).
CONSIDER: *v.t.*, tingim; *v.i.*, harim long liwa.
CONSTABLE: *n.*, (native) polisboi; polisman, siutman.
CONSULT: *v.t.*, askim.
CONSUME: *v.t.*, kaikai, pinisim.
CONTENT: *a.*, orait.
CONTINUE: *v.i.*, wok, stap yet.
CONTRACT: *n.*, kontrak (of service), peipa.
CONVICT: *n.*, kalabus.
COOK: *n.*, kuk, kukboi; *v.t.*,. COOKED- dan, dan pinis. In parts of New Britain, "kuk" also means wife.
COOL: *a.*, kol liklik.
COPRA: *n.*, kopra.
COPULATE: *v.i.*, puspus. C. with- goapim *(v.t.)*.
CORAL: *n.*, rip; CORAL RUBBLE- granas.
CORD: *n.*, rop, twain.
CORK: *n.*, ai, kok, tuptup.
CORN: *n.*, kon; on sole of foot – tampilua, tono. WILD CORN- karapai.
CORRECT: *a.*, stret; *v.t.*, stretim.
CORRIDOR: *n.*, pasis.
CORRODE: *v.t.*, kaikai.
COST: *n.*, pei.
COSTLY: *a.*, dia, dia tumas.
COTTON: *n.*, katen. COTTON WOOL- kepok.
COUCH: *n.*, bet.
COUGH: *n.*, and *v.i.*, kus.
COULD: *v.i.*, inap long. COULD BE- aitingk.
COUNT: *v.t.*, kauntim.
COUNTERPART: *n.*, proman.
COUNTRY: *n.*, ples. Definitely not kandere.
COUNTRYMAN: *n.*, wantok.
COUPLE: *n.*, tupela.
COURSE: *n.*, rot. OF COURSE!- nau wonem!

COURT: *n.*, Kot, Haus Kot; *v.t.*, grisim, gris long; TAKE TO COURT- kotim.
COURTEOUS: *a.*, naispela.
COUSIN: *n.*, barata or sisa as case may be. See P.39.
COVER: *v.t.*, karamap; *n.*, tuptup.
COVET: *v.t.*, mangal long.
COW: *n.*, bulmakau meri; *v.t.*, pretim.
COWER: *v.i.*, surik.
COWRIE SHELL: *n.*, girigiri.
COY: *a.*, sem.
CRAB: *n.*, kuka; HERMIT CRAB- katu.
CRACKLE: *v.i.*, pairap.
CRANE: *n.*, winis; (bird) longpela nek.
CRAVE: *v.t.*, dai long.
CRAWL: *v.i.*, wokabaut long bel.
CRAYFISH: *n.*, kindam, kropis.
CRAZY: *a.*, longlong.
CREAM: *n.*, strongpela susu.
CREATE: *.t.*, bringim, wokim, gerapim.
CREEK: *n.*, liklik wara.
CREEP: *v.i.*, stil.
CRESS: *n.*, kangko.
CREW: *n.*, boskru.
CRIME: *n.*, rong.
CRIMINAL: *n.*, man nogut.
CRIPPLED: *a.*, skruilus.
CROCODILE: *n.*, pukpuk.
CROOKED: *a.*, kronggut, no stret.
CROSS: *n.*, diwai kros; *a.*, kros.
CROW: *n.*, kotkot (bird), krai bilong kokoruk; *v.i.*, kokoruk i krai.
CROWBAR: *n.*, kroba.
CROWD: *v.i.*, and *n.*, bung; *v.t.*, bungim: CROWDED- i pa.
CRUCIFIX: *n.*, Diwai Kros.
CRUEL: *a.*, hat tumas, sakman.
CRUMBS: *n.*, pipia bilong bret.
CRUSH: *v.t.*, krunggutim, nogut.
CRY: *v.i.*, kraikrai, krai; *n.*, krai.
CUCUMBER: *a.*, kukamba.
CULTIVATION: *n.*, wok.
CUP: *n.*, kap. Half coconut shell- BILO.
CURE: *v.t.*, oraitim.
CURRENT: *n.*, tait.
CURRY: *n.*, kari.

CURSE: *v.t.,* toknogutim.
CURVE: *v.t.,* kronggutim: *v.i.,* raun.
CUSCUS: *n.,* kapul.
CUSTARD: *n.,* kasta.
CUSTOM: *n.,* pasin, lo.
CUSTOMS: *n.,* Kastans.
CUT: *v.t.,* katim; *n.,* sua.
CUTTER: *n.,* (boat) kata.
CUTTLEFISH: *n.,* tauka.
CYCLE: *v.i.,* ron long wilwil.
CYLINDER: *n.,* paip.

DAILY: *adv.,* long ol de; oltaim long de.
DAINTY: *a.,* naispela.
DALLY: *v.i.,* langsam, hambag.
DAMAGE: *v.t.,* bagarapim, brukim.
DAMP: *a.,* kol.
DANCE: *v.i.,* samsam, singsing; *n.,* singsing.
DANGLE: *v.i.,* hanggimap.
DARK: *a.,* and *n.,* tudak.
DARN: *v.t.,* soimap.
DATE: *n.,* de.
DAUGHTER: *n.,* pikinini meri.
DAWDLE: *v.i.,* langsam.
DAWN: *n.,* moningtaim tru, hap tulait.
DAY: *n.,* tulait, de, san.
DAYLIGHT: *n.,* tulait.
DAZED, BE: *a.,* longlong, ai i raun.
DEAD: *a.,* dai pinis.
DEADLY: *a.,* samting bilong mekim dai man.
DEAF: *a.,* yaupas.
DEAR: *a.,* (costly) dia.
DEATH: *n.,* dai.
DEBATE: *n.,* wokurai; *v.t.,* wokurai long.
DEBT: *n.,* dinaur. BE INDEBTED TO (OWE)- dinaur long ...
DECAY: *v.i.,* stink.
DECEIT: *n.,* giaman.
DECEIVE: *v.t.,* giamanim.
DECEMBER: *n.,* Desemba.
DECK: *n.,* antek; *v.t.,* bilasim.
DECLARE: *v.i.,* tok, tok i spik.
DECOMPOSE: *v.i.,* stink.
DECORATE: *v.t.,* bilasim.

DECOY: *v.t.,* giamanim.
DECREE: *n.,* lo.
DECREPIT: *a.,* lapun, as melum melum.
DEEP: *a.,* daun tumas, daun.
DEFEAT: *v.t.,* winim, daunim, win long.
DEFEND: *v.t.,* sambai long ... halivim. DEFENDANT- wetkot.
DEFICIENT: *a.,* no inap; DEFICIENT IN- nogat.
DEFLECT: *v.t.,* sakim.
DEFLOWER: *v.t.,* bagarapim.
DELUDE: *v.t.,* giamanim.
DEMENTED: *a.,* longlong.
DEMOLISH: *v.t.,* bagarapim, brukim.
DEMON: *n.,* masalai.
DEMONSTRATE: *v.t.,* makim, soim.
DEMUR: *v.i.,* no laik.
DENSE: *a.,* i pas.
DENTIST: *n.,* dokta bilong tis.
DENY: *v.t.,* tok nogat.
DEPART: *v.i.,* go, gerap i go.
DEPOSIT: *v.t.,* putim.
DEPRIVE: *v.t.,* pulim, tekewe.
DEPUTY: *n.,* tultul.
DERMATITIS: *n.,* grili.
DERRICK: *n.,* winis.
DESCEND: *v.i.,* go daun, kam daun.
DESCENDANT: *n.,* pikinini; tumbuna pikinini.
DESERT: *v.i.,* ronewe; *n.,* ples nogut; ston na waitsan tasol.
DESIGN: *n.,* mak.
DESIGNATE: *v.t.,* soim, makim.
DESIRE: *v.t.,* laikim; *n.,* laik.
DESIST: *v.t.,* pinis long.
DESPISE: *v.t.,* no laikim
DESPITE: *prep.,* maski.
DESPOT: *n.,* sakman.
DESSERT: *n.,* switkai.
DESTITUTE: *a.,* rabis.
DESTROY: *v.t.,* bagarapim.
DETECT: *v.t.,* painim.
DETOUR: make a ... raun.
DEVASTATE: *v.t.,* bagarapim.
DEVIL: *n.,* Masalai, Satan.
DEVOID: *a.,* nogat.
DEVOUR: *v.t.,* kaikai.

DEW: *n.*, kol.
DIARRHOEA, to have; pekpek wara.
DIE: *v.i.*, dai; dai pinis.
DIESELINE: *n.*, disil.
DIFFERENT: *a.*, narakain.
DIG: *v.t.*, brukim (graun).
DILIGENT, be: *a.*, save wok strong.
DINNER: *n.*, kaikai. More specifically – kaikai bilong nait, apinun.
DIRECT: *a.*, stret; *v.t.*, soim. DIRECTIONS- toksave.
DIRTY: *a.*, doti, no klin. See DOTI.
DISABLE: *v.t.*, bagarapim.
DISAPPEAR: *v.i.*, lus olgeta.
DISCARD: *v.t.*, tromwe.
DISCLOSE: *v.t.*, telimaut; mekim kamap.
DISCORD: *n.*, kros.
DISCOURSE: *n.*, orovasio.
DISCOVER: *v.t.*, painim pinis.
DISCREET: *a.*, isi; *adv.*, isi.
DISCUSS: *v.t.*, warkurai long.
DISCUSSION: *n.*, warkurai.
DISEASE: *n.*, sik.
DISEMBARK: *v.i.*, go daun.
DISGRACE: *n.*, sem; be disgraced- gat sem.
DISH: *n.*, dis.
DISH OUT: *v.t.*, dilim.
DISHONESTY: *n.*, pesin bilong stil.
DISINFECTANT: *n.*, stink maresin.
DISLIKE: *v.t.*, nolaik, nolaikim.
DISMISS: *v.t.*, rausim.
DISOBEY: *v.t.*, sakim tok.
DISORDERED: *a.*, hipnabaut.
DISPENSARY: *n.*, haus marasin.
DISPLAY: *v.t.*, soim, lainim.
DISPUTE: *n.*, and *v.i.*, kros.
DISRESPECT: *n.*, bighet.
DISSEMBLE: *v.i.*, giaman.
DISTANT: *a.*, longwe.
DISTRIBUTE: *v.t.*, dilim.
DISTRICT: *n.*, hap; ples.
DISTRICT COMMISSIONER: *n.*, disi. D. OFFICER- Nambawan Kiap.
DITCH: *n.*, barat.
DIVIDE: *v.t.*, hapim; divide out- dilim.
DIVORCE: *v.t.*, rausim; brukim marit.

DIVULGE: *v.t.*, telimaut; mekim kamap.
DO: *v.i.*, mekim. DO NOT MATTER- maski. DO NOT- yu no ..., maski long ...
DOCK: *n.*, draidok.
DOCTOR: *n.*, dokta.
DOCUMENT: *n.*, peipa; pas.
DODGE: *v.t.*, abrisim; *v.i.*, abris.
DOG: *n.*, dok.
DOG FISH: *n.*, sak anggau.
DOLT: *n.*, nasau.
DOMESTIC SERVANT: *n.*, mankimasta.
DONKEY: *n.*, donki; esel.
DOOR: *n.*, dua.
DOVE: *n.*, liklik balus.
DOWN: *adv.*, daun; *n.*, mosong (fine hairs, etc.).
DRAG: *v.t.*, pulim.
DRAIN: *n.*, barat.
DRAW: *v.t.*, wokim piksa.
DRAWER: *n.*, rum (bilong bokis klos, etc.).
DREAD: *n.*, pret.
DREAM: *n.*, and *v.i.*, driman.
DRESS: *n.*, klos; *v.i.*, putim klos.
DRIER (copra): *n.*, haus smok.
DRILL: *n.*, boa; (military) sasait; *v.t.*, borim.
DRINK: *n.*, dring; *v.t.*, dringim.
DRIVER: *n.*, draivaboi, draiva.
DROUGHT: *n.*, bikpela san.
DROWN: *v.i.*, lus long wara; dring wara pinis.
DROWSY, BE: *a.*, dai long slip, ai hevi.
DRUG: *n.*, maresin.
DRUM: *n.*, kundu; garamut.
DRUNK: *a.*, longlong long wiski.
DRY: *a.*, drai, draipela.
DUCK: *n.*, pato.
DUE: *n.*, dinaur (debt).
DUGONG: *n.*, bulmakau bilong solwara; bonon.
DUMB: *a.*, nek i pas, maus pas.
DUNG: *n.*, pekpek.
DURING: *prep.*, long, long taim bilong.
DUSK: *n.*, klosap tudak.
DWELL: *v.i.*, stap.
DUTY: *n.*, wok.
DYE: *n.*, pen; *v.t.*, penim.

DYNAMITE: *n.,* patron, dainamait.
DYSENTERY, to have: pekpek blut.

EACH: *a.,* wanpela wanpela.
EAGER: *a.,* hat.
EAGLE: *n.,* tarangau; manigulai (sea eagle).
EAR: *n.,* yau.
EARLY: *a.,* and *adv.,* (in the day) moningtaim tru, long tulait; (in the afternoon) klosap bihain long belo; (in time) pastaim i nupela yet; (action) pas; (state) state time of day, week, etc.
EARRING: *n.,* ring bilong yau, kalong.
EARTH: *n.,* graun; Daun.
EARTHQUAKE: *n.,* guria.
EAST: *adv.,* long hap bilong san i gerap.
EASY: *a.,* isi; no hatwok.
EAT: *v.i.,* and *v.t.,* kaikai, kaikaim.
EBB TIDE: *n.,* draiwara.
EDGE: *n.,* arere.
EDIBLE: *a.,* gutpela bilong kaikai.
EDICT: *n.,* lo.
EDUCATE: *v.t.,* lainim.
EEL: *n.,* mario; SALTWATER EEL- tuna.
EFFEMINATE: *a.,* (of a man) nainsi.
EFFIGY: *n.,* devel.
EGG: *n.,* kiau.
ELBOW: *n.,* skru.
ELDER: *n.,* lapun; bikpela man.
ELECT: *v.t.,* makim.
ELEGANT: *a.,* naispela.
ELEVEN: *num.,* wanpela ten wan.
ELF: *n.,* tambaran.
ELOPE: *v.i.,* ronewe.
ELUDE: *v.t.,* ronewe long; abrisim.
EMACIATED: *a.,* bun nating.
EMBARGO: *n.,* tambu.
EMBARRASS: *v.t.,* semim.
EMBARRASSMENT: *n.,* sem.
EMBLEM: *n.,* mak; namba.
EMINENT: *n.,* bikpela (man).
EMPLOY: *v.t.,* wok long (hammer, etc.); BE EMPLOYED BY- wok long ...
EMPLOYER: *n.,* masta.
EMPLOYMENT: *n.,* wok.

EMPTY: *a.*, anti; ... nating. Bokis nating- EMPTY BOX.
ENCHANTMENT: *n.*, malira; papait.
ENCIRCLE: *v.t.*, banisim.
ENCLOSURE: *n.*, banis.
END: *v.i.*, pinis; *v.t.*, pinisim.
ENEMY: *n.*, birua.
ENGINE: *n.*, masin, ensin.
ENGINEER: *n.*, ansini.
ENGLISH: *n.*, Inglis. Also ENGLAND: *a.*, bilong Inglis.
ENJOY: *v.t.*, laikim tumas.
ENORMOUS: *a.*, draipela; bikpela.
ENOUGH: *a.*, inap.
ENRAGED, BE: belihat.
ENTER: *v.t.*, go nisait long ...
ENTICE: *v.t.*, pulim; grisim.
ENTIRE: *a.*, olgeta.
ENTRAILS: *n.*, bel.
ENUMERATE: *v.t.*, kauntim.
ENVELOPE: *n.*, ambilok, skinpas.
ENVIOUS: *a.*, mangal.
ENVY: *n.*, mangal.
EPIDEMIC: *n.*, bikpela sik.
EPSOM SALTS: *n.*, solmarasin.
EQUAL: *a.*, inap. EQUAL TO- inap long.
ERODE: *v.t.*, kaikai.
ERROR, BE IN: longlong.
ESCAPE: *v.i.*, ronewe.
ETERNAL: *a.*, bilong oltaim.
EUCALYPT: *n.*, kumurere.
EURASIAN: *n.*, Hapkas.
EUROPEAN: *n.*, Masta.
EVADE: *v.t.*, abrisim; ronewe long ...
EVEN: *a.*, stret; klin.
EVENING: *n.*, apinun.
EVENTUALLY: *adv.*, baimbai.
EVER: *adv.*, oltaim.
EVERY: *a.*, ol; olgeta.
EVERYBODY: *n.*, ol manmeri.
EVICT: *v.t.*, rausim.
EVIL: *a.*, nogut.
EXACTLY: *adv.*, stret.
EXAMPLE: *n.*, GIVE AN EXAMPLE OF- soim kain.
EXCELLENT: *a.*, gutpela, namba wan.

EXCEPT: *prep.,* tasol.
EXCESSIVE: *a.,* tumas.
EXCHANGE: *v.t.,* senisim, halivim.
EXCITE: *v.t.,* kirapim bel bilong ...
EXCRETA: *n.,* pekpek.
EXEMPT: *v.t.,* larim.
EXERCISE: *n.,* sasait.
EXHAUSTED: *a.,* sotwin.
EXHIBIT: *v.t.,* soim; lainim.
EXIST: *v.i.,* stap.
EXPAND: *v.t.,* solapim; *v.i.,* solap.
EXPECT: *v.t.,* wetim; ting bai ... (expect something to happen).
EXPEL: *v.t.,* rausim i raus.
EXPENSIVE: *a.,* dia tumas.
EXPLODE: *v.i.,* pairap.
EXTREMELY: *adv.,* tru.
EYE: *n.,* ai; mata kiau – having ONE EYE.

FABLE: *n.,* tok kuskus.
FACE: *n.,* no general term. Use nus, maus, asket, etc. See *PES*.
FACTORY: *n.,* haus wok, (e.g., CIGARETTE FACTORY- haus wok bilong tabak).
FAD: *n.,* wisis.
FAECES: *n.,* pekpek.
FAINT: *v.i.,* dai; ai i raun.
FAIRY: *n.,* tambaran; FAIRY TALE- tok kuskus.
FAITH: *n.,* bilip.
FALL: *v.i.,* pundaun.
FALSE: *a.,* giaman; lai.
FALSEHOOD: *n.,* giaman.
FAMILIAR WITH, BE: save gut long.
FAMILY: *n.,* lain.
FAMINE: *n.,* taim bilong hanggre.
FAMOUS: *a.,* gat nem.
FANCY: *n.,* wisis, ting.
FANG: *n.,* tis.
FAR: *a.,* longwe.
FART: *n.,* and *v.i.,* puinga, kapopo.
FARTHER: *a.,* longwe moa.
FAST: *adv.,* kwik; *a.,* kwikpela; pas, strong.
FASTEN: *v.t.,* pasim.
FAT: *a.,* pat, bikbel, bikpela; *n,* gris.
FATALITY: *n.,* birua.

FATHER: *n.*, papa. PRIEST- Pater.
FATHOM: *n.*, pram.
FAULT: *n.*, rong, trabel.
FEAR: *n.*, pret; *v.t.*, pret long.
FEAST: *n.*, kaikai; GIVE A FEAST- mekim kaikai.
FEATHER: *n.*, gras (bilong pisin).
FEBRUARY: *prop.n.*, Februari.
FEE: *n.*, pe.
FEED: *v.t.*, givim kaikai.
FEEL: *v.t.*, pilim; holim.
FEIGN: *v.i.*, giaman.
FEINT at: *v.t.*, giamanim.
FELLOW: *n.*, proman.
FEMALE: *a.*, and *n.*, meri.
FENCE: *n.*, banis; *v.t.*, banisim.
FERN: *n.*, pulpul.
FESTER: *v.i.*, stink.
FESTIVAL: *n.*, singsing.
FETCH: *v.t.*, kisim (i kam).
FEUD: *n.*, kros.
FEVER: *n.*, fiva, skin i hat.
FEW: *a.*, i no planti, wan wan.
FIBRE: *n.*, tret.
FICTION: *n.*, giaman.
FIG: *n.*, fikas.
FIGHT: *n.*, pait; *v.i.*, pait; pait long- FIGHT WITH. See PAITIM.
FIGURE: *n.*, namba; mak.
FILCH: *v.t.*, stilim.
FILE: *n.*, pait; *v.t.*, pailim.
FILL: *v.t.*, fulimap.
FILTHY: *a.*, doti tumas.
FIND: *v.t.*, painim pinis.
FINE: *a.*, liklik; BE FINED- baiim kot.
FINGER: *n.*, pinga. FINGERNAIL- kapa.
FINISH: *v.t.*, pinisim; *n.*, pinis.
FIRE: *n.*, paia.
FIREARMS: *n.*, masket.
FIREWORKS: *n.*, pauda.
FIRM: *a.*, pas; strong.
FIRST: *a.*, nambawan, paslain long; *adv.*, pastaim.
FISH: *n.*, pis; *v.i.*, huk. See Fish in classified vocab. p.65.
FISH HOOK: *n.*, huk.
FIT: *v.t.*, inapim; *a.*, inap.

FIX: *v.t.,* wokim, mekim orait gen.
FLAG: *n.,* plak.
FLAME: *n.,* paia; *v.t.,* lait bikpela.
FLARE: *n.,* bumbum.
FLASH: *v.i.,* pairap; *a.,* bilas.
FLASHLIGHT: *n.,* siutlam.
FLAT: *a.,* stret; (tyre) i slek.
FLATTER: *v.t.,* grisim.
FLATTERY: *n.,* gris.
FLEA: *n.,* laus.
FLEE: *v.i.,* ronewe.
FLESH: *n.,* mit.
FLIRT: *v.i.,* hambak.
FLOAT: *v.i.,* drip; *v.t.,* suimim.
FLOG: *v.t.,* paitim.
FLOOD: *n.,* tait; BE IN FLOOD- gat tait.
FLOOR: *n.,* plo.
FLOUR: *n.,* plaua.
FLOUT: *v.t.,* sakim.
FLOWER: *n.,* pulpul, plaua. OF THE COCONUT PALM- nok.
FLY: *n.,* lang; *v.i.,* flai, ran antap.
FLYING FOX: *n.,* blakbokis.
FOG: *n.,* smok, klaud.
FOLD: *v.t.,* brukim
FOLLOW: *v.t.,* bihainim; *v.i.,* kam bihain.
FOLLY: *n.,* kranki, longlong.
FOOD: *n.,* kaikai.
FOOL: *n.,* kranki man, blatiful, pulman.
FOOLISH: *a.,* kranki, longlong.
FOOLISHNESS: *n.,* hambak.
FOOT: *n.,* lek.
FOOTBALL: *n.,* kikbal.
FOOTPATH: *n.,* rot.
FOOTPRINT: *n.,* leg.
FOR: *prep.* and *conj.,* bilong (purpose); long.
FORBID: *v.t.,* tambuim.
FORE: *a.,* bilong pas.
FOREARM: *n.,* han.
FOREFATHER: *n.,* tumbuna.
FOREHEAD: *n.,* pes.
FOREST: *n.,* bus.
FOREVER: *adv.,* bilong oltaim.
FORGET: *v.t.,* lusim.

FORGIVE: *v.t.*, larim.
FORK: *n.*, pok; GARDEN FORK- gabel.
FORLORN: *a.*, taronggu.
FORMER: *a.*, bilong bipo.
FORMERLY: *adv.*, bipo, bipotaim.
FORNICATE: *v.i.*, ple, puspus.
FORSAKE: *v.t.*, lusim olgeta.
FORWARD: *adv.*, pas; long pas.
FOWL: *n.*, kakaruk, paul. WILD FOWL- wail paul, paul bilong bus.
FRAGILE: *a.*, no strong.
FRAGRANCE: *n.*, gutpela smel.
FRAIL: *a.*, no strong.
FRANK, BE: tok tru, noken haitim.
FRAUD: *n.*, giaman.
FRAY: *n.*, pait; *v.i.*, skrap; *v.t.*, skrapim.
FREE: *v.t.*, lusim; *a.*, nogat pe long em; GOT FREE- ronewe.
FRENCH: *prop.a.* and *pron.*, Pranis.
FREQUENT: *a.*, planti taim. Also adverb.
FRESH: *n.*, nupela, klin, klinpela.
FRIDAY: *n.*, Fraide.
FRIEND: *n.*, pren.
FRIGHTEN: *v.t.*, pretim, mekim pret.
FRIGHTENED: *a.*, pret.
FROCK: *n.*, klos.
FROG: *n.*, rokrok.
FROLIC: *n.*, ple.
FROM: *prep.*, long
FROND: *n.*, bombom.
FRUIT: *n.*, prut. There is no real generic term for fruit.
FRY: *v.t.*, praim.
FRYPAN: *n.*, praipan.
FULL: *a.*, pulap.
FUN: *n.*, ple.
FUNNEL: *n.*, paip.
FUNNY: *a.*, bilong lap.
FUR: *n.*, gras.
FURIOUS: *a.*, kros tumas.
FURL: *v.t.*, brukim.
FURTHER: *adv.*, longwei moa.
FUSE: *n.*, pius.
FUTURE: *n.*, taim bihain.

GAFF: *n.,* kap.
GALE: *n.,* bikpela win.
GALLANTLY: *adv.,* gutpela tumas, strong tumas.
GALVANISED IRON: *n.,* kapa.
GAMBOL: *n.* and *v.i.,* ple.
GAMBLE: *v.i.,* ple laki.
GAME: *n.,* ple.
GANG: *n.,* lain.
GAOL: *n.,* kalabus.
GAR: *n.,* longpela maus.
GARAGE: *n.,* haus motakar.
GARBAGE: *n.,* pipia.
GARDEN: *n.,* wok; gaten. Wok is usual.
GARFISH: *n.,* longpela maus.
GARMENT: *n.,* klos; laplap.
GAS: *n.,* win.
GATE: *n.,* doa.
GATHER: *v.t.,* kisim, putim wantaim, bungim.
GAUDY: *a.,* bilas tumas.
GAUZE: *n.,* gos.
GAZE: *v.i.,* lukluk.
GENEROUS: *a.,* gutpela; i no dia.
GENIAL: *a.,* gutpela.
GENITALS: *n.,* kan, bokis (f); kok (m).
GENUINE: *a.,* tru.
GEOLOGIST: *n.,* masta bilong lukim ston.
GERMAN: *n.,* Siaman.
GET: *v.t.,* kisim.
GHOST: *n.,* devel.
GIDDY: *a.,* ai i raun.
GIFT: *n.,* presen.
GIMLET: *n.,* liklik boa.
GINGER: *n.,* kawawar (the wild variety mostly).
GIRL: *n.,* pikinini meri, meri.
GIVE: *v.t.,* givim.
GLAD, BE: hamamas, bel bilong (mi) i orait.
GLANCE: *n.,* lukluk.
GLARE: *v.i.,* lait strong.
GLASS: *n.,* glas; EYEGLASSES- aiglas.
GLEAM: *v.i.,* lait.
GLISTEN: *v.i.,* lait.
GLOAT: *v.i.,* tok bilas.
GLOOM: *n.,* tudak.

GLUE: *n.,* laim; *v.t.,* laimim.
GNAT: *n.,* natnat.
GNAW: *v.t.,* kaikai.
GO: *v.i.,* go.
GOANNA: *n.,* palai.
GOAT: *n.,* me.
GOD: *n.,* Deo.
GOLD: *n.,* golmoni.
GOLDLIP SHELL: *n.,* kina, golip.
GONE: *a.,* go pinis; (with inanimate noun) i lus (lost or stolen).
GONG: *n.,* belo; WOODEN G.- garamut.
GOOD: *a.,* gutpela.
GOODBYE: *v.i.* and *n.,* gutbai.
GOODS: *n.,* kago.
GOSPEL: *n.,* evangelio.
GOSH: *excl.,* olaboi! olaman!
GOOSE: *n.,* patogus.
GOSSIP: *n.,* gris; tokwin.
GOURA PIGEON: *n.,* guria.
GOURD: *n.,* skin kambong.
GOVERNMENT: *n.,* gauman.
GOVERNOR: *n.,* Nambawan Gauman.
GOWN: *n.,* klos.
GRAND: *a.,* bikpela.
GRANDFATHER: *n.,* tumbuna; GRANDMOTHER is also TUMBUNA. Use either "papa" or "mama" as a qualifier.
GRAPEFRUIT: *n.,* bikpela muli.
GRASP: *v.t.,* holimpas, holim strong.
GRASS: *n.,* gras; blady grass- kunai.
GRASS KNIFE: *n.,* sarip.
GRATE: *v.t.,* skrapim.
GRAVE: *n.,* matmat.
GRAVEL: *n.,* granas.
GRAVY: *n.,* greve.
GRAZE: *v.t.,* boinim (with bullet or arrow); kaikai gras (cattle).
GREASE: *n.,* gris, *v.t.,* putim gris long, grisim.
GREASY: *a.,* wel.
GREAT: *a.,* bikpela.
GREEDY: *a.,* mangal.
GREEN: *a.,* grin, grinpela, blupela.
GRIEF: *n.,* sori.
GRIEVE: *v.i.,* sori.
GRIM: *a.,* kros.

GRIN: *v.i.,* lap.
GRIP: *v.t.,* holim strong.
GROAN: *v.i.,* krai.
GROPER: *n.,* draipela bikpela maus.
GROUND: *n.,* graun.
GROUP: *n.,* lain; *v.t.,* bungim.
GROVE: *n.,* lain (ex. lain kokonas).
GRUB: *n.,* liklik snek.
GUARD: *n.,* gad; was; *v.t.,* was long ...
GUAVA: *n.,* yambo.
GUIDE: *v.t.,* bringim; soim.
GUILE: *n.,* giaman, gris.
GUITAR: *n.,* gita.
GULL: *n.,* kanai; *v.t.,* giamanim.
GULLY: *n.,* barat.
GUM: *n.,* laim; *v.t.,* laimim.
GUN: *n.,* masket; GAN PISIN- shotgun; HAN GUN- pistol.
GUNPOWDER: *n.,* pauda.
GUTTER: *n.,* barat.

HABIT: *n.,* pasin.
HAIR: *n.,* gras.
HALF: *n.,* hap stret, haphap.
HALFCASTE: *n.,* hapkas.
HALLOWED: *a.,* takondo.
HALVE: *v.t.,* haphapim, brukim namel.
HALYARD: *n.,* halias.
HAMMER: *n.,* hama; *v.t.,* hamarim.
HAMPER: *n.,* basket; *v.t.,* pasim.
HAND: *n.,* han.
HANDCUFF: *n.,* hankas.
HANDLE: *n.,* stik; *v.t.,* holim.
HANDSOME: *a.,* naispela.
HANG: *v.t.,* hanggimapim; *v.i.,* hanggimap.
HAPLESS: *a.,* taronggu.
HAPPY: *a.,* bel i gutpela; hamamas.
HARBOUR: *n.,* ples bilong anka; *v.t.,* haitim.
HARD: *a.,* hat; strong, hatpela.
HARDSHIP: *n.,* hatwok.
HARLOT: *n.,* pamuk.
HARMFUL: *a.,* (samting) nogut.
HASTEN: *v.i.,* hariap; *v.t.,* hariapim.
HAT: *n.,* hat.

HATCH: *v.t.,* kakarim.
HATCHES: *n.,* asis.
HAVE: *v.t.,* gat; *aux.v.,* bin. HAVE TO- mas.
HAVERSACK: *n.,* brasben.
HAWK: *n.,* taranggau.
HAZE: *n.,* smok.
HE: *pers.pr.,* em.
HEAD: *n.,* het.
HEADACHE, TO HAVE: het i pen.
HEADDRESS: *n.,* kangal.
HEADLAND: *n.,* poin.
HEADWATERS: *n.,* ai bilong wara.
HEADMAN: *n.,* Luluai.
HEAL: *v.t.,* mekim gut gen.
HEAR: *v.t.,* harim.
HEART: *n.,* pam.
HEAT: *v.t.,* hotim; *n.,* hat.
HEATHERN: *n.,* tematan.
HEAVE: *v.t.,* torome. HEAVE HO!- haisa lo!
HEAVEN: *n.,* Antap, Heven.
HEAVY: *a.,* heve.
HEED: *v.t.,* harim gut.
HELL: *n.,* Imperno.
HELM: *n.,* stia.
HELP: *v.t.,* halpim.
HEM: *n.,* arere.
HEN: *n.,* paul, kokoruk meri.
HER: *pers.pr.,* em; *poss.pr.*- bilong em.
HERE: *adv.,* hia.
HEREAFTER: *adv.,* bihain.
HERMIT CRAB: *n.,* katu.
HERON: *n.,* longpela nek.
HERRING: *n.,* malambul.
HERSELF: *p.,* em yet.
HIDE: *v.i.,* hait; *v.t.,* haitim, karamapim; *n.,* skin.
HIGH: *a.,* antap.
HIGH TIDE: *adv.,* haiwara.
HIGHWAY: *n.,* rot, bikrot.
HILL: *n.,* mauntin.
HINDER: *v.t.,* pasim.
HINGE: *n.,* ain.
HIRE: *v.t.,* baim.
HIS: *poss.p.,* bilong em.

HIT: *v.t.,* paitim, slapim; HIT VERY HARD- kilim.
HOAX: *v.t.,* giamanim.
HOE: *n.,* baira.
HOIST: *v.t.,* haisim.
HOLD: *n.,* (ship's) bikdaunbilo; *v.t.,* holim.
HOLE: *n.,* hul.
HOLIDAY: *v.i.,* limlimbu; *n.,* de bilong limlimbu.
HOLY: *a.,* takondo.
HOME: *n.,* ples; haus.
HONE: *n.,* ston; *v.t.,* sapim.
HONEY: *n.,* hani, suga bilong binatang.
HONOUR: *v.t.,* hamamas long ..., beten long ...
HOOK: *n.,* huk; *v.t.,* hukim.
HORN: *n.,* kom; CONCH SHELL- taul.
HORNBILL: *n.,* kokomo.
HORSE: *n.,* hos.
HOSE: *n.,* paip (gumi).
HOSPITAL: *n.,* haus sik.
HOT: *a.,* hat, hatpela.
HOTEL: *n.,* haus dringk.
HOUR: *n.,* aua.
HOUSE: *n.,* haus.
HOUSEBOY: *n.,* mankimasta.
HOW: *adv.,* olsem wonem; HOW MUCH- haumas; HOW MANY- haumas; HOW MANY TIMES-haumas taim.
HOWL: *v.i.,* karai.
HUDDLE: *v.i.,* bung.
HUMBLE: *a.,* rabis.
HUNDRED: *num.,* hundet.
HUNGER: *n.,* hanggre.
HUNGRY: *a.,* hanggre.
HUNT: *v.t.,* ronim; *v.i.,* go siut, go painim (wailpik, pisin, etc.).
HUNTER: *n.,* (employed) siutboi.
HURRICANE: *n.,* bikpela win.
HURRY: *v.i.,* hariap; *v.t.,* hariapim.
HURT: *v.i.,* pen; *v.t.,* bagarapim.
HUSBAND: *n.,* man.
HUSK: *n.,* skin; *v.t.,* tekewe skin.
HUT: *n.,* haus.
HYMN: *n.,* singsing bilong lotu.

I: *pers.p.,* mi.
ICE: *n.,* ais.

IDEA: *n.*, ting.
IDIOT: *n.*, longlong man.
IDLE: *a.*, bilong les; *v.i.*, les.
IF: *conj.*, tasol; sapos.
IGNITE: *v.t.*, laitim.
IGNORANT: *a.*, longlong. BE I.- no save.
IGUANA: *n.*, palai.
ILL: *a.*, sik.
ILLNESS: *n.*, sik.
IMAGE: *n.*, devel.
IMITATE: *v.t.*, bihainim pasin bilong ...
IMMEDIATELY: *adv.*, nau.
IMPASSABLE: *a.*, pas.
IMPEDE: *v.t.*, pasim.
IMPERTINENCE: *n.*, bighet.
IMPERTINENT: *a.*, bighet; seki.
IMPORTANT: *a.*, bikpela; samting tru.
IMPOSSIBLE, BE: no ken tru.
IMPRISON: *v.t.*, kalabusim.
IMPRUDENT: *a.*, longlong; kranki; nogat ting.
IMPUDENT: *a.*, seki.
IN: *prep.*, long, nisait long.
INACCURATE: *a.*, no stret, giaman.
INACTIVE: *a.*, nating.
INADEQUATE: *a.*, no inap.
INCAPABLE: *a.*, no inap; no ken.
INCITE: *v.t.*, gerapim.
INCLINE: *v.i.*, lintaun.
INCONSISTENT, BE: tanim gen, faulnabaut.
INCORRECT: *a.*, no stret; giaman, kranki.
INDEBTED: *a.*, dinaur.
INDEED: *adv.*, nau wonem! tru.
INDICATE: *v.t.*, soim ... long.
INDIFFERENT: *a.*, les.
INDIGNANT, BE: gerap nogut.
INDISCREET: *a.*, longlong.
INDOLENT: *a.*, les.
INDUCE: *v.t.*, grisim, pulim.
INEFFECTIVE: *a.*, no inap.
INEXPERT: *a.*, heve, no save gut.
INEXTRICABLE: *a.*, paulnabaut, pasnabaut.
INFANT: *n.*, pikinini.
INFECTED: *a.*, stink. INFECTION- sua, sik. INFECTED WITH- gat ...

INFERIOR: *n.,* ananit, daun. I. TO- no inap long ...
INFIDEL: *n.,* tematan.
INFIRM: *a.,* lapun, no strong.
INFLATED, BE: solap.
INFLUENCE: *v.t.,* tanim tingting bilong ...
INFORM: *v.t.,* tokim; selim tok long ...
INFRINGE: *v.t.,* skrapim.
INHABIT: *v.t.,* stap long ...
INJECTION: *n.,* siut; TO HAVE AN I- kesim nil.
INK: *n.,* ing; tinte.
INLAND: *adv.,* long bus.
INLET: *n.,* pasis.
INNOCENT: *a.,* no gat rong.
INQUIRE: *v.t.,* and *v.i.,* askim.
INSANE: *a.,* longlong.
INSECT: *n.,* binatang.
INSECURE: *a.,* no pas gut; no strong.
INSIDE: *prep.,* nisait long ..., *adv.,* nisait.
INSIST: *v.i.,* strong.
INSOLENCE: *n.,* bighet. INSOLENT- seki.
INSPECT: *v.i.,* lukim.
INSTRUCT: *v.t.,* lainim, skulim.
INSTRUCTIONS: *n.,* toksave.
INSUFFICIENT: *a.,* no inap.
INSULT: *v.t.,* toknogutim.
INTELLIGENT: gat save, bilong save.
INTEND: *aux.v.,* laik.
INTERIOR: *n.,* nisait.
INTERPRET: *v.t.,* tanim tok; INTERPRETER- savitok.
INTERROGATE: *v.t.,* askim.
INTERRUPT: *v.t.,* brukim tok.
INTO: *prep.,* long; nisait long ...
INVALID: *n.,* sikman; *a.,* no inap, pinis.
INVEIGLE: *v.t.,* grisim.
INVESTIGATE: *v.t.,* wok save long ...
INVINCIBLE: *a.,* strong.
IODINE: *n.,* aiadin, yot.
IRASCIBLE: *a.,* kros.
IRON: *n.,* ain; GALVANISED IRON- kapa.
IS: *v.i.,* see BE.
ISLAND: *n.,* ailan.
IT: *pron.,* em. ITS- bilong em.
ITALIAN: *prop.a.,* and *pron.,* Pranis.

ITCH: *v.i.,* skrap.
ITEM: *n.,* samting.
ITSELF: *pron.,* em yet.

JACARANDA: *n.,* maramal.
JAM: *n.,* siam.
JANUARY: *n.,* Januari.
JAPANESE: *a.,* Siapan.
JAUNT: *n.,* limlimbu.
JAW: *n.,* askit.
JEALOUS: *a.,* mangal.
JEER: *v.i.,* tok bilas.
JERSEY: *n.,* kol singlis.
JEST: *n.,* ple.
JET: (airplane) *n.,* boing.
JETTY: *n.,* bris.
JEW: *prop.n.,* Juda.
JEW'S HARP: *n.,* susap.
JIB: (Naut.) *n.,* kliwa.
JIB-BOOM: (Naut.) *n.,* sibum.
JOB: *n.,* wok.
JOIN: *v.t.,* skruim, pasim wantaim.
JOINT: *n.,* skru.
JOKE: *v.i.,* ple; *n.,* tok ple.
JOY: *n.,* hamamas.
JUDGE: *n.,* biksuds; *v.t.,* (legal) harim kot long ...; tingim.
JUG: *n.,* jak.
JUICE: *n.,* wara.
JULY: *n.,* Julai.
JUMP: *v.i.,* kalap; *v.t.,* kalapim.
JUNE: *n.,* Jun.
JUNGLE: *n.,* bikbus.
JUST: *a.,* stret; tasol (only).

KANGAROO; *n.,* sikau; TREE KANGAROO- sikau bilong diwai.
KAPOK TREE: *n.,* kepok.
KEDGE: *n.,* anka.
KEEL: *n.,* kil.
KEEP: *v.t.,* holim; stap long ... - KEPT BY ...
KEROSENE: *n.,* kerosin.
KETTLE: *n.,* ketel.
KEY: *n.,* ki.
KHAKI: *a.,* kaki.
KICK: *v.t.,* kikim; *v.i.,* kik- KICK, PLAY FOOTBALL.

KID ALONG: *v.t.,* grisim.
KILL: *v.t.,* mekim dai.
KIND: *a.,* gutpela.
KINDRED: *n.,* lain, pisin.
KING: *n.,* King.
KITBAG: *n.,* kikbek.
KITCHEN: *n.,* haus kuk.
KNAPSACK: *n.,* ruksak.
KNEE: *n.,* skru (bilong lek).
KNIFE: *n.,* naip.
KNOB: *n.,* buk.
KNOCK ON: *v.t.,* paitim.
KNOT: *n.,* buk; *v.t.,* pasim.
KNOW: *v.t.,* save long ...
KNOWLEDGE: *n.,* save.
KNUCKLE: *n.,* skru bilong pinga.

LABEL: *n.,* namba.
LABOUR: *v.i.* and *n.,* wok.
LABOURER: *n.,* wokboi.
LACK: *v.t.,* no gat.
LAD: *n.,* manki.
LADDER: *n.,* lata.
LADLE: *n.,* bikpela spun, bilo (half coconut shell).
LAG: *v.i.,* langsam.
LAGOON: *n.,* raunwara.
LAKE: *n.,* raunwara.
LAME: *a.,* skruilus.
LAMP: *n.,* lam.
LAMPBLACK: *n.,* sit bilong lam.
LANCE: *n.,* spia.
LAND: *n.,* graun; *v.i.,* pundaun (to alight), kam sua (come ashore).
LANDS OFFICE: *n.,* Haus Lain.
LANE: *n.,* rot; pasis.
LANGUAGE: *n.,* tok.
LANKY: *a.,* longpela nating.
LANTERN: *n.,* lam. HURRICANE LANTERN- lam wokabaut.
LARD: *n.,* gris bilong pik.
LARDER: *n.,* stua.
LARGE: *n.,* bikpela.
LAST: *a.,* bihain tru.
LATE: *a.,* bihain.
LAUGH: *v.i.,* lap.

LAUNCH: *n.,* pinas, kata.
LAVATORY: *n.,* haus pekpek, smol haus.
LAW: *n.,* lo; LAWSUIT- kot; BREAK THE L.- skrapim lo.
LAX: *a.,* slek.
LAY: *v.t.,* putim, slipim.
LAZINESS: *n.,* les.
LAZY: *a.,* les.
LEAD: *n.,* bol.
LEAD: *v.t.,* bringim, go paslain.
LEAF: *n.,* lip.
LEAN: *v.i.,* lintaon; *a.,* bun nating.
LEAP: *v.i.,* kalap; *v.t.,* kalapim.
LEARN: *v.t.,* lainim, lain long, skul long.
LEATHER: *n.,* let.
LEAVE: *n.,* limlimbu; *v.t.,* lusim i stap; GIVE LEAVE- orait long; DEPART FROM- lusim.
LECTURE: *n.,* oratovo.
LEECH: *n.,* snek.
LEFT: *a.,* kais, leptan. LEFT HAND- hankais, leptan.
LEG: *n.,* lek.
LEGEND: *n.,* tok kuskus.
LEMON: *n.,* muli.
LEMONADE: *n.,* lemone.
LEND: *v.t.,* gipim pastaim.
LENIENT: *a.,* no had; gutpela.
LENT: *n.,* Viniwel.
LEPROSY: *n.,* tamata, kempe, tabak.
LET OFF: *v.t.,* larim; LET GO- legoim *(v.t.)*; LET BE- larim i stap.
LETTER: *n.,* pas.
LEVEL: *a.,* stret.
LEWD: *a.,* pamuk, nogut.
LIANA: *n.,* rop bilong bus.
LIAR: *n.,* man bilong giaman; lai.
LICE: ngos ngos.
LICENCE: *n.,* laisin.
LID: *n.,* hat, tuptup.
LIE: *v.i.* and *n.,* giaman; lai.
LIE: *v.i.,* slip.
LIFT: *v.t.,* litimapim, haisapim.
LIGHT: *n.,* lam, lait; *v.t.,* laitim; *a.,* no heve.
LIKE: *v.t.,* laikim; *a.,* olsem.
LIMB: *n.,* han.
LIME: *n.,* kambang; (fruit) muli, siporo.

LIMIT: *n.,* arere.
LINE: *v.t.,* lainim; *v.i.,* lain; *n.,* lain. FORM A LINE- polain.
LINEN: *n.,* laplap.
LINT: *n.,* ling.
LISTEN: *v.i.,* harim.
LITTLE: *a.* and *n.,* liklik.
LIVE: *v.i.,* stap.
LIVER: *n.,* liva.
LIZARD: *n.,* palai.
LOAD: *n.,* kago; *v.t.,* putim kago.
LOAFER: *n.,* lesman.
LOAN: *n.,* dinaur.
LOBSTER: *n.,* kindam. There are none in New Guinea – they are crayfish.
LOCATE: *v.t.,* painim.
LOCK: *n.,* lok; *v.t.,* lokim.
LOG: *n.,* diwai.
LOITER: *v.i.,* langsam; hambag.
LONE: *a.,* wanpela.
LONG: *a.,* longpela; *v.i.,* (LONG FOR ...) dai long ..., sotwin long ..., krai long ...
LOOK: *v.i.,* lukluk; LOOK AT- lukim, lukluk long ..., LOOK FOR- painim.
LOOKING GLASS: *n.,* glas lukluk.
LOOSE: *v.t.,* lusim; *a.,* slek; LOOSEN- slekim.
LOST: *a.,* lus pinis.
LOT: *n.,* ol.
LOUD: *a.,* strong.
LOUSE: *n.,* ngos ngos.
LOVE: *v.t.,* laikim tumas. LOVER- pren.
LOW: *a.,* daun.
LOWER: *v.t.,* slekim daun isi.
LOWLAND: *n.,* ples daun.
LUBRICATE: *v.t.,* putim wel long, putim gris long, welim.
LUFF: *v.i.,* lapap.
LUGGAGE: *n.,* kago.
LUNCH: *n.,* belo kaikai.
LUNG: *n.,* waitliva.
LURE: *v.t.,* grisim, pulim, giamanim.
LURK: *v.i.,* stil, hait.

MACHINE: *n.,* masin.
MACKEREL: *n.,* dangil.

MAD: *a.,* longlong.
MADNESS: *n.,* longlong.
MAGGOT: *n.,* liklik snek.
MAGIC: *n.,* poisin, puripuri (from Pidgin Motu).
MAGISTRATE: *n.,* kiap.
MAID: *n.,* yangpela meri.
MAIL: *n.,* mel.
MAILBAG: *n.,* begmel.
MAIN: *a.,* namba wan. MAINSAIL- mensel.
MAINLAND: *n.,* bikples.
MAIZE: *n.,* kon.
MAKE: *v.t.,* wokim. Cf., mekim.
MALAY: *n.,* Krani.
MALE: *a.,* man.
MAN: *n.,* man.
MANAGER: *n.,* namba wan.
MANDARIN: *n.,* sotpela swit muli.
MANGROVE: *n.,* manggros; kolsis (a small leafed variety).
MANGO: *n.,* manggo.
MANNER: *n.,* pasin.
MANY: *a.,* planti.
MAP: *n.,* kat.
MARCH: *prop.n.,* Mas; *v.i.,* kwikmas.
MARGIN: *n.,* arere.
MARK: *n.,* mak; *v.t.,* makim.
MARKET: *n.,* bung.
MARMOT: *n.,* mumut.
MARRIAGE: *n.,* marit.
MARRY: *v.t.,* maritim. UNMARRIED- yangpela, skelman.
MARSH: *n.,* ples melum melum.
MARSUPIAL RAT: *n.,* mumut.
MARTINET: *n.,* sakman.
MASH: *v.t.,* paitim.
MASS: *n.,* Misa.
MAST: *n.,* mas.
MASTER: *n.,* masta.
MAT: *n.,* mat.
MATCHES: *n.,* masis; STRIKE MATCH- slekim masis.
MATE: *n.,* poroman, pren.
MATTER, DOESN'T: maski.
MATTOCK: *n.,* marik.
MATURE: *a.,* man; bikpela pinis.
MAY: *n.,* Mai.

ME: *pers.p.,* mi.
MEAL: *n.,* kaikai.
MEANDER: *v.i.,* snek nabaut.
MEASURE: *n.,* mesa; *v.t.,* skelim.
MEAT: *n.,* abus, mit.
MECHANIC: *n.,* ansini.
MEDAL: *n.,* mendal.
MEDICAL ASSISTANT; *n.,* Liklik Dokta.
MEDICAL ORDERLY: *n.,* doktaboi.
MEDICINE: *n.,* marasin.
MEDITATE: *v.i.,* ruru.
MEET: *v.t.,* painim, kamap long ...
MEETING: *n.,* kivung.
MELODY: *n.,* musik.
MELON: *n.,* melen.
MEMORIZE: *v.t.,* lainim gut.
MEND: *v.t.,* wokim gen.
MENSTRUATE: *v.i.,* karim blut.
MERCY: *n.,* marimari; HAVE MERCY ON- marimari long ...
MERELY: *adv.,* tasol.
MESSAGE: *n.,* tok, wailis.
METAL: *n.,* ain.
METHYLATED SPIRITS: *n.,* spiris.
MIDDAY: *n.,* twelklok, belo kaikai.
MIDDLE: *n.,* namil.
MIDGE: *n.,* natnat.
MIDNIGHT: *a.,* biknait.
MIDWAY: *n.,* namil.
MILK: *n.,* susu. MILKFISH- susu.
MILL: *n.,* haus masin (see sawmill).
MIND: *n.,* liva, tingtingk.
MINDFUL, BE: ting long ...; no lusim ...
MINE: *poss.pro.,* bilong mi.
MINER: *n.,* masta bilong wokim golmoni.
MIRE: *n.,* giraun melum melum.
MIRROR: *n.,* glas lukluk.
MISBEHAVE: *v.i.,* hambak.
MISCHIEF: *n.,* hambak.
MISCONDUCT: *n.,* pasin nogut, rong.
MISDEED: *n.,* rong, trabel.
MISREPORT: *v.i.,* giaman.
MISS: *v.t.,* popaia long; *v.i.,* popaia (generally a target or objective); dai long ...

MISSIONARY: *n.,* misin.
MIST: *n.,* klaut, smok.
MISTER: *n.,* Masta.
MISTRANSLATE: *v.t.,* tanim kranki, tanim-gen.
MISTRESS: *n.,* pren; *q.v.,* misis.
MIX: *v.t.,* abusim, tanim wantaim.
MOCK: *v.t.,* tok bilas long ...
MODEST: *a.,* sem.
MODESTY: *n.,* sem.
MOIST: *a.,* kol.
MONDAY: *n.,* Mande.
MONEY: *n.,* moni.
MONKEY: *n.,* monki.
MONOPLANE: *n.,* wanwing.
MONSOON: *n.,* N.W.- tolo. S.E.- rai.
MONTH: *n.,* mun.
MOON: *n.,* mun.
MORE: *adv.,* and *a.,* moa.
MORNING: *n.,* moning, moningtaim.
MOROSE: *a.,* kros.
MORTGAGE: *n.,* dinaur.
MOSQUITO: *n.,* maskita. MOSQUITO NET- taunem, klambu.
MOTHER: *n.,* mama.
MOTOR: *n.,* ensin, masin.
MOTOR BOAT: *n.,* pinas.
MOTORCAR: *n.,* motaka.
MOUNTAIN: *n.,* maunten; MOUNTAINOUS- i gat maunten.
MOURN: *v.t.,* sori long.
MOUSE: *n.,* liklik rat.
MOUSTACHE: *n.,* mausgras.
MOUTH: *n.,* maus.
MOUTH ORGAN: *n.,* musik.
MOVE: *v.t.,* pulim ... i kam (towards); siubim ... i go (away from); *v.i.,* meknais.
MUCH: *a.,* planti.
MUD: *n.,* graun melum melum.
MULE: *n.,* donki.
MULLET: *n.,* karua.
MURDER: *n.,* birua; *v.t.,* kilim birua, birua long ...; MURDERER-kilman.
MUSCLE: *n.,* mit.
MUSHROOM: *n.,* kru bilong graun, talinga, papai.
MUSIC: *n.,* musik.
MUST: *aux.v.,* mas.

MUTE: *a.,* nek i pas, maus pas. See NONG.
MUTTON: *n.,* sip-sip, mit bilong sip-sip.
MUZZLE: *n.,* maus.
MY: *poss.pr.,* bilong mi.
MYSELF: *pron.,* mi yet.
MYTH: *n.,* tok kuskus.

NAIL: *n.,* nil.
NAME: *n.,* nem; *v.t.,* kolim nem bilong ..., givim nem long ...
NARROW: *a.,* liklik.
NATIVE: *n.,* native of – man bilong. Use the proper noun of the tribe or nation.
NATURAL: *a.,* olsem (after the noun).
NAUSEA, HAVE: laik traut.
NEAR: *adv.,* klostu.
NEARLY: *adv.,* klosap.
NEAT: *a.,* stret, naispela.
NECK: *n.,* nek.
NECKLACE: *n.,* bis.
NEEDLE: *n.,* nil. SAILMAKER'S NEEDLE- pamnil.
NEEDY: *a.,* rabis.
NEGATIVE: *adv.,* nogat; *a.,* nating.
NEGLECT: *v.t.,* lusim, no ting long ...; *n.,* hambak.
NEPHEW: *n.,* pikinini; nephew of maternal uncle – kandere.
NERVOUS: *a.,* guria.
NEST: *n.,* haus bilong pisin, kokoruk, etc.
NET: *n.,* umben; mosquito net – taunem, klambu; net bag – bilum.
NETTLE: *n.,* sarat.
NEW: *a.,* nupela.
NEW GUINEA: *prop.n.,* Nu Gini.
NEWS: *n.,* tok.
NEWSPAPER: *n.,* niuspeper.
NIGHT: *n.,* tudak, nait.
NIGHT DRESS: *n.,* klos slip.
NIPA: *n.,* marota.
NIPPLE: *n.,* ai bilong susu.
NO: *adv.,* nogat. BY NO MEANS- nogat tru.
NOBLE: *n.,* man i gat nem.
NOISE: *n.,* meknais.
NONE: *a.* and *pron.,* nogat.
NORTHWEST TRADES: *n.,* taleo.
NOSE: *n.,* nus.
NOT: *neg.,* no.

151

NOTE: *v.t.*, lukim gut; *n.*, pas; **PAPER MONEY**- konda moni.
NOTHING: *n.*, nogat samting. Vide grammar, p.15.
NOTION: *n.*, ting.
NOVEMBER: *n.*, Nowemba.
NOW: *adv.*, nau.
NUMB: *a.*, i dai.
NUMBER: *n.*, namba.
NUMERALS: See chapter XI.
NUMEROUS: *a.*, planti, pulap long.
NUN: *n.*, sista.
NURSE: *n.*, sista, misis dokta.
NUT: *n.*, see bilinat, galip, kasang, kasta, kawiwi, kokonas, okari, talasa, talis.

OAF: *n.*, longlong man, nasau.
OAR: *n.*, pul.
OBEY: *v.t.*, harim tok.
OBJECT: *n.*, samting; *v.i.*, no laik.
OBLIGATION: *n.*, dinaur (monetary).
OBSCENE: *a.*, nogut.
OBSERVE: *v.t.*, lukim gut.
OBSIDIAN: *n.*, botol.
OBSTRUCT: *v.t.*, pasim.
OBTAIN: *v.t.*, kisim.
OCCUPY: *v.t.*, stap long.
OCEAN: *n.*, solwara.
OCTOBER: *n.*, Octoba.
OCTOPUS: *n.*, urita.
ODOUR: *n.*, smel.
OF: *prep.*, bilong.
OFFENCE: *n.*, rong.
OFFICER: *n.*, Is an officer – i gat namba. See Didiman, Dokta, Kastans, Kiap, Polismasta.
OFFICIAL: *n.*, **VILLAGE OFFICIAL**- Luluai (head), tultul (asst.), Doktaboi (medical orderly); *a.*, tok bilong kiap, tok bilong gavman.
OFTEN: *adv.*, planti taim.
OH: *excl.*, oleboi! oleman!
OIL: *n.*, wel; *v.t.*, putim wel long, welim.
OILY: *a.*, wel.
OINTMENT: *n.*, gris.
OLD: *a.*, lapun, olpela. **OLD PERSON**- lapun.
OMIT: *v.t.*, lusim.
ON: *prep.*, long.

ONCE: *adv.*, bipotaim; *num.a.*, wanpela taim.
ONE: *num.a.*, wanpela; *card.num.*, wan.
ONION: *n.*, anian.
ONLY: *a.*, tasol.
OPEN: *v.t.*, opim; *a.*, op.
OPINION: *n.*, ting.
OPOSSUM: *n.*, kapul.
OPPOSITE: *adv.*, hapsait
OR: *conj.*, olosem.
ORANGE: *n.*, swit muli.
ORDER: *v.t.*, tokim; IN ORDER THAT- bilong, bai.
ORGANISE: *v.t.*, (dance, etc.) gerapim.
ORIGIN: *n.*, as.
ORNAMENT: *n.*, bilas.
OSPREY: *n.*, manigulai.
OTHER: *a.*, arapela.
OUGHT: *v.i.*, mas.
OUR: *poss.pr.*, bilong mipela (or yumi).
OURSELVES: *pr.*, mipela yet, yumi yet.
OUTRIGGER: *n.*, saman.
OUTSIDE: *n.*, arasait; *a.*, arasait long.
OVEN: *n.*, aven. See MUMU.
OVER: *prep.*, antap long.
OVERCAST, BE; (klaut) i pas.
OVERFLOW: *v.i.*, kapsait.
OVERPOWER: *v.t.*, daunim em holimpas.
OVERSEER: *n.*, bos, bosboi.
OVERTURN: *v.i.*, kapsait; *v.t.*, kapsaitim.
OWE: *v.t.*, gat dinaur long.
OWNER: *n.*, papa bilong ... See p.57.
OX: *n.*, bulmakau.
OYSTER: *n.*, kina, wusta.

PACK: *v.t.*, putim long bokis, pasim; *n.*, ruksak (army).
PADDLE: *v.i.* and *n.*, pul.
PAGAN: *n.*, tematan.
PAGE: *n.*, lip, pagina.
PAIL: *n.*, baket.
PAIN: *n.*, pen. PAINFUL- im i pen.
PAINT: *n.*, pen; *v.t.*, penim.
PAIR: *n.*, tupela. ONE OF A P.- proman.
PALM: *n.*, nisait long han; SAILMAKER'S P.- pamlil; P. TREES- see baibai, kokonas, kawiwi, bilinat, limbong, saksak.

PAN: *n.*, praipan.
PANDANUS: *n.*, hum, karuka, marita.
PANT: *v.i.*, pulim win; PANT AFTER- sotwin long ...
PANTRY: *n.*, stua.
PAPER: *n.*, pepa; PAPER MONEY- konda moni.
PARADISE, BIRD OF: *n.*, kumul.
PARASOL: *n.*, ambrela.
PARCEL: *n.*, karamap, mekpas.
PARDON: *v.*, larim.
PARE: *v.t.*, sapim; tekwe skin.
PARROT: *n.*, marip, klangal (large green and red parrot).
PART: *n.*, hap.
PARTNER: *n.*, proman.
PARTY, POLITICAL: *n.*, pati.
PASS: *n.*, (leave, permit) pas; *v.t.*, go pas long ...
PASSION, BE IN A: belihat.
PAST: *a.*, bipo; *n.*, bipotaim; *adv.*, pas; bilong bipo – IN THE PAST.
PATCH: *v.t.*, somapim, sodarim (vulcanize or solder).
PATH: *n.*, rot.
PATIENT: *n.*, sikman; *a.*, isi.
PATROL: *v.i.*, wokbus: PATROL OFFICER- Kiap.
PAUPER: *n.*, rabisman.
PAUSE: *v.i.*, wet pastaim, malalo.
PAW: *n.*, han.
PAWPAW: *n.*, popo.
PAY: *v.t.*, baim, gipim pe long ...; *n.*, pe.
PEACE: *n.*, (absence of fighting) taim bilong sikan. BE AT P.- stapgut.
PEANUT: *n.*, galip bilong graun, kasang.
PEARL: *n.*, kiau bilong kinya.
PEARLSHELL: *n.*, kinya.
PEAS: *n.*, hebsen.
PEDAL: *n.*, tirap; *v.t.*, kikim.
PEEL: *v.t.*, tekewe skin; *n.*, skin.
PEN: *n.*, pen.
PENCIL: *n.*, pensil, kirip.
PENIS: *n.*, kok.
PENKNIFE: *n.*, naip skru.
PEOPLE: *n.*, ol, ol manmeri.
PEPPER: *n.*, pepa. WILD PEPPER *(piper betel)*- daka.
PERCEIVE: *v.t.*, save; lukim.
PERFORM: *v.t.*, mekim.
PERFUME: *n.*, santa.
PERHAPS: *adv.*, aiting.

PERIOD: *n.,* taim.
PERISH: *v.i.,* lus.
PERMIT: *n.,* pas, laisen; *v.t.,* larim.
PEROXIDE: *n.,* proksait.
PERSON: *n.,* wanpela, man.
PERSONALLY: *adv.,* yet.
PERSPIRE: *v.i.,* skin i wara, tuhat i kamap. PERSPIRATION- tuhat.
PERSUADE: *v.t.,* grisim, pulim.
PETROL: *n.,* bensin.
PHOTOGRAPH: *n.,* poto, piksa.
PICK: *n.,* pik; *v.t.,* pikim (graun); makim (choose).
PICTURE: *n.,* piksa.
PIDGIN ENGLISH: *n.,* Tok Pisin, Tok Boi.
PIECE: *n.,* hap, liklik hap.
PIER: *n.,* bris.
PIERCE: *v.t.,* siutim.
PIG: *n.,* pik.
PIGEON: *n.,* balus; LARGE CRESTED PIGEON- guria.
PIKE: *n.,* spia; (a fish) malisa.
PILLOW: *n.,* pilo; WOODEN HEAD REST- kaluk.
PILOT: *n.,* stiaman; (of a plane) kepten bilong balus.
PIN: *n.,* nil.
PINCERS: *n.,* sangge, kuka.
PINE: *n.,* (tree) plangk.
PINE FOR: sori long.
PINEAPPLE: *n.,* painap, ananas.
PINK: *a.,* ret.
PINNACE: *n.,* pinas, kata.
PIPE: *n.,* paip, mambu.
PISTOL: *n.,* liklik masket, han gun.
PIT: *n.,* hul.
PITCH: *n.,* kol ta.
PITEOUS: *a.,* kalopa.
PITH: *n.,* meme.
PITIFUL: *a.,* kalopa.
PITY: *v.i.,* marimari long.
PLACE: *n.,* hap; *v.t.,* putim.
PLANE: *n.,* hobel (carpenter).
PLANK: *n.,* plank.
PLANT: *v.t.,* plantim; *n.,* pulpul.
PLATE: *n.,* plet.
PLATFORM: *n.,* bed.
PLAY: *v.i.,* ple; PLAY CARDS- ple kas.

PLAYGROUND: *n.,* ples ple.
PLEASE: *v.t.,* grisim; wok long grisim em – set out to please him.
PLENTY: *a.,* planti.
PLIERS: *n.,* plaias.
PLUME: *n.,* kangal; gras bilong pisin.
POCKET: *n.,* bak; TROUSERS POCKET- bak trausis.
POINT TO or AT: *v.t.,* soim, makim long han.
POISON: *n.,* gip.
POLICEMAN: *n.,* siutman; NATIVE POLICE- polisboi.
POLICE OFFICER: *n.,* plismasta, masta plis.
POLISH: *n.,* metal polish – polis; leather polish – kiwi; *v.t.,* polisim.
POLITE: *a.,* naispela.
POND: *n.,* raunwara.
POOL: *n.,* raunwara.
POOR: *a.,* rabis.
POPE: *n.,* Papa.
PORK: *n.,* pik.
PORPOISE: *n.,* ambusa, popis.
PORT SIDE: *n.,* bekbot.
PORTION: *n.,* hap; *v.t.,* skelim, dilim.
PORTRAIT: *n.,* piksa.
POSSESS: *v.t.,* gat.
POSSIBLY: *adv.,* aiting.
POSSUM: *n.,* kapul.
POST: *n.,* pos.
POST OFFICE: *n.,* haus pos.
POSTPONED, BE: i stap pastaim.
POT: *n.,* sospen.
POTATO: *n.,* potete. SWEET POTATO- kaukau.
POULTRY: *n.,* kokoruk, faul.
POUR: *v.t.,* kapsaitim.
POWDER: *n.,* kampang smel.
POWER: *n.,* strong; POWERFUL: *a.,* strongpela.
POWERHOUSE: *n.,* haus masin.
PRACTICE: *v.i.,* sasaet. See *pasin,* p.101.
PRAISE: *v.t.,* beten long.
PRAWN: *n.,* liklik kindam.
PRAY: *v.i.,* raring.
PRAYER: *n.,* raring.
PREACH: *v.i.,* orovasio.
PRECEDE: *v.t.,* go pas long ...
PREFER: *v.t.,* laikim.
PREGNANT: *a.,* gat bel.

PREPARE: *v.t.*, rediim.
PREPARED, BE: sambai, redi.
PRESENT: *n.*, presen; *v.t.*, (present arms) – presen; presen long em.
PRESENTLY: *adv.*, liklik taim.
PRESSURE LAMP: *n.*, lam bensin.
PRESTIGE: *n.*, nem, strong.
PRETENCE: *n.*, giaman.
PRETEND: *v.i.*, giaman.
PRETTY: *a.*, naispela; PRETTILY: *adv.*, nais.
PREVENT: *v.t.*, pasim.
PREVIOUS: *a.*, bilong pastaim; *adv.*, bipo.
PRIMUS STOVE: *n.*, pranis.
PRICE: *n.*, pe.
PRIEST: *n.*, prista, pater.
PRINT: *v.t.*, paitim long masin.
PRIOR: *a.*, bilong pastaim; *adv.*, pastaim long ...
PRISON: *n.*, kalabus.
PRISONER: *n.*, kalabus.
PROBABLY: *adv.*, aiting.
PROCEDURE: *n.*, pasin.
PROCURE: *v.t.*, go kisim.
PRODUCE: *v.t.*, bringim.
PROFANITY: *a.*, tok nogut.
PROHIBIT: *v.t.*, tambuim.
PROHIBITION: *n.*, tambu.
PROMPT: *a.a*, kwik.
PROPEL: *v.t.*, siubim.
PROPELLER: *n.*, kropela.
PROPERTY: *n.*, samting.
PROSTITUTE: *n.*, meri pamuk; TRAVELLING PROSTITUTE- pasensa meri.
PROTECT: *v.t.*, was long ..., sambai long ...
PROTEST: *v.i.*, gerap nogut.
PROTESTANT: *n.*, Talatala.
PUGNACIOUS: *a.*, bilong pait.
PULL: *v.t.*, pulim.
PULLEY: *n.*, blok.
PUMP: *n.*, pam.
PUMPKIN: *n.*, pamken.
PUNCH: *v.t.*, tromwe han long ...
PUNCTURE: *v.t.*, siubium.
PUNISH: *v.t.*, paitim, mekim sore.
PUNY: *a.*, bun nating.

PUPIL: *n.,* sumatin, skulboi.
PURCHASE: *v.t.,* baim.
PURGATORY: *prop.n.,* Purgatorio.
PURPLE: *a.,* ret.
PURSE: *n.,* liklik paus bilong moni.
PURSUE: *v.t.,* ronronim.
PUS: *n.,* susu.
PUSH: *v.t.,* siubim.
PUT: *v.t.,* putim.
PUTRID: *a.,* stingk.
PUTTY: *n.,* kit.
PYJAMAS: *n.,* klos slip.
PYTHON: *n.,* moran.

QUACK: *n.,* krai bilong pato.
QUAKE: *n.* and *v.i.,* guria.
QUALITY: *n.,* pasin.
QUANTITY: *n.,* sampela.
QUARREL: *v.i.,* mekim kros, tok kros.
QUARTER: *n.,* haphapim na hap.
QUARTERS: *n.,* haus; MEN'S QUARTERS- hausboi.
QUEEN: *prop.n.,* Kwin.
QUEER: *a.,* narakain.
QUESTION: *v.t.,* askim.
QUIBBLE: *v.i.,* hambag.
QUICK: *a.,* kwik.
QUICKLY: *adv.,* kwiktaim; kwik, hariap.
QUIET: *a.,* stap nating, no meknais; *adv.,* isi.
QUININE: *n.,* kinin.
QUIT: *v.t.,* lusim olgeta.
QUOTE: *v.t.,* makim tok bilong ....

RABBIT: *n.,* pusi. This is how they look in the freezer, however.
RACE: *n.,* resis; (mining) barat; *v.i.,* resis.
RADIO: *n.,* wailis.
RAG: *n.,* pipia lap-lap.
RAIN: *n.,* ren; *v.i.,* ren i kam daun; BE RAINING- ren i stap.
RAINCOAT: *n.,* kot ren.
RAISE: *v.t.,* litimapim, sanapim, haisim.
RAMBLE: *v.i.,* gokambaut, limlimbu.
RANT: *v.t.,* bikmaus nating.
RAPE: *v.t.,* bagarapim, pulim, duim, stilim.
RAT: *n.,* rat.
RATION: *n.,* skel.

RATTAN: *n.*, kanda.
RATTLE: *n.*, salamon; *v.i.*, meknais.
RAVAGE: *v.t.*, bagarapim.
RAVEN: *n.*, kotkot.
RAW: *a.*, no tan, amat.
RAY: *n.*, (fish) epa.
RAZOR: *n.*, resa; RAZOR BLADE- kapa resa.
READ: *v.t.*, kauntim; *v.i.*, rit.
READY: *a.*, redi. BE READY- sambai.
REAL: *a.*, tru.
REALIZE: *v.i.*, save.
REALLY: *adv.*, tru.
REAR: *n.*, bihain, baksait.
REBUKE: *v.t.*, krosim.
RECEIVE: *v.t.*, kisim.
RECENT: *a.*, nau tasol.
RECITE: *v.t.*, kauntim.
RECLINE: *v.i.*, slip.
RECLUSE: *n.*, wanpis.
RECOGNIZE: *v.t.*, luksave long ...
RECOIL: *v.i.*, surink. Of a rifle – kik.
RECOLLECT: *v.t.*, harim, harim gen long liva.
RECOMPENSE: *v.t.*, baim, bekim.
RECORD: *n.*, plet musik; *v.t.*, putim ... long pepa.
RECOVER: *v.t.*, kisim bek; *v.i.*, orait gen.
RECRUIT: *n.*, krutman; *v.t.*, baim boi.
RECTIFY: *v.t.*, stretim.
RED: *a.*, red, retpela.
REEF: *n.*, rip.
REFLECTION: *n.*, dewel.
REFRIGERATOR: *n.*, bokis ais.
REFUSE: *n.*, meme, pipia.
REGAIN: *v.t.*, kisim bek.
REGARD: *v.t.*, lukim; HIGH REGARD- laikim tumas.
REGION: *n.*, hap.
REGRET: *v.t.*, sori long; *n.*, sori.
REGULATION: *n.*, loa.
REJECT: *v.t.*, tromwe, rausim bek.
RELATE: *v.t.*, tokim.
RELATIVE: *n.*, wan lain.
RELEASE: *v.t.*, lusim, legoim.
RELIEVE: *v.t.*, halivim.
RELIGION: *n.*, lotu.

RELUCTANT: *a.*, nolaik, les long.
REMAIN: *v.i.*, stap.
REMEMBER: *v.t.*, holim long ting ting.
REMNANT: *n.*, hap i stap.
REMOTE: *a.*, longwe tumas.
REMOVE: *v.t.*, tekewe, rausim.
REND: *v.t.*, brukim.
REPAIR: *v.t.*, wokim gen, mekim orait gen.
REPAST: *n.*, kaikai.
REPAY: *v.t.*, bekim.
REPEAT: *v.t.*, mekim gen, tokim gen.
REPEL: *v.t.*, rausim bek.
REPENT: *v.i.*, nukpuku.
REPLACE: *v.t.*, halivim, putim i go bek, kesim ples bilong ...
REPLY: *n.*, bekim; *v.i.*, bekim tok i spik.
REPORT: *v.t.*, tokim (kiap, etc.) long ...
REPOSE: *v.t.*, slipim; *v.i.*, slip.
REPRIMAND: *v.t.*, krosim.
REPTILE: *n.*, snek.
REPULSE: *v.t.*, rausim bek.
REQUEST: *v.t.*, askim.
RESEMBLE: *v.t.*, lukluk olosem.
RESENT: *v.t.*, nolaik tru.
RESIDE: *v.i.*, stap.
RESIDUE: *n.*, meme.
RESOLUTE: *a.*, strong.
RESPITE: *n.*, malolo.
RESPOND: *v.i.*, bekim tok i spik.
REST: *n.* and *v.i.*, malolo, kesim win.
RESTORE: *v.t.*, givim bek.
RETAIN: *v.t.*, holim, pasim.
RETICENT: *a.*, no tok, nong.
RETINUE: *n.*, lain.
RETREAT: *v.i.*, ronewe.
RETRIEVE: *v.t.*, kisim bek.
RETURN: *v.i.*, kam bek; go bek.
REVEAL: *v.t.*, mekim kamap, telimautim.
REVENGE: *v.t.*, bekim.
REVERSE: *v.i.*, gostan (ship and car).
REVOLVER: *n.*, liklik masket, han gan.
REWARD: *n.*, pe; *v.t.*, baim.
RIBS: *n.*, banis. R. OF COCONUT LEAF- bun.
RICE: *n.*, rais.

RIDGE: *n.,* kil.
RIFLE: *n.,* masket, raifel.
RIGGING: (Naut.) *n.,* riken.
RIGHT: *a.,* stret; RIGHT-HAND- hansiut, raithan.
RIGID: *a.,* strong.
RIM: *n.,* arere.
RING: *n.,* ring.
RINGLEADER: *n.,* paslain.
RINGWORM: *n.,* grile.
RIPE: *a.,* mau.
RISE: *v.i.,* gerap, sanap.
RITE: *n.,* singsing, lainim.
RIVER: *n.,* riva, wara: RIVER MOUTH- lek bilong wara: HEADWATERS- ai bilong wara.
ROAD: *n.,* rot.
ROAM: *v.i.,* gokambaut.
ROAST: *v.t.,* kukim long paia, kukim long aven (bake).
ROB: *v.t.,* pulim samting bilong ... ROBBER- stilman.
ROBUST: *a.,* strong.
ROCK: *n.,* ston. See SIPRAM.
ROLL: *v.t.,* tantanim i ron; ROLL UP- lotim; *n.,* (of material) lot.
ROOF: *n.,* generally translated by calling it by what it's made of, e.g., kapa, saksak.
ROOM: *n.,* rum.
ROOSTER: *n.,* kokoruk man.
ROOT: *n.,* rop; as; *v.i.,* mumut: ROOT FOR- mumutim.
ROPE: *n.,* rop, lain, baklain. KRAKON- a bush vine used as rope.
ROSARY BEADS: *n.,* kurkurua.
ROT: *v.i.,* stingk. ROTTEN- stingk.
ROUND: *a.,* raun, raunpela.
ROUSE: *v.t.,* gerapim.
ROW: *n.,* lain; *v.i.,* pul long bot (kanu); *v.t.,* pulim.
RUB: *v.t.,* rapim.
RUBBER: *n.,* gumi.
RUBBISH: *n.,* pipia.
RUBBLE: *n.,* granas.
RUCKSACK: *n.,* ruksak.
RUDDER: *n.,* stia.
RUDE PERSON: *n.,* buskanaka.
RUG: *n.,* mat, blangket.
RUIN: *v.t.,* bagarapim.
RULE: *n.,* loa.
RUM: *n.,* ram.

RUMOUR: *n.*, tok wailis.
RUMP: *n.*, as.
RUN: *v.i.*, ron, ronigo; *v.t.*, ronronim.
RUST: *n.* and *v.i.*, ros.
RUSTLE: *v.i.*, meknais.

SACK: *n.*, bek; *v.t.*, rausim.
SACRED: *a.*, takondo, tambu, santu.
SAD: *a.*, sori, bel i nogut.
SADDLE: *n.*, sarel.
SAFE, FOOD: *n.*, bokis kaikai.
SAGO: *n.*, saksak.
SAIL: *n.*, sel. MAINSAIL- mensel. See also KLIWA.
SAILFISH: *n.*, selpis.
SAILOR: *n.*, sela, boskru.
SAINT: *n.*, Takondo.
SALARY: *n.*, pe.
SALIVA: *n.*, spet.
SALT: *n.*, sol.
SAME: *n.*, im tasol; *a.*, wan-, e.g., wankain- SAME SORT; wanples- SAME VILLAGE, etc.
SAND: *n.*, waitsan.
SANDFLY: *n.*, natnat.
SANDPAPER: *n.*, sampepa.
SANITARY: *a.*, mumut (i.e., dealing with cleansing services); klin, klinpela.
SAP: *n.*, blut.
SARDINES: *n.*, talai (tin talai).
SASH: *n.*, pus.
SATAN: *n.*, Satan, Masalai.
SATISFACTORY: *a.*, orait.
SATURDAY: *n.*, Sarere.
SAUCE: *n.*, sos, greve.
SAUCEPAN: *n.*, sospen.
SAUCY: *a.*, seki.
SAUSAGE: *n.*, sosis.
SAVAGE: *n.*, wailman, manambus, buskanaka.
SAVELOY: *n.*, sosis.
SAVOUR: *v.t.*, traiem; *n.*, smel.
SAW: *n.*, so; *v.t.*, soim.
SAWDUST: *n.*, pipia bilong so.
SAWFISH: *n.*, sopis.
SAWMILL: *n.*, haus masin plang.

SAY: *v.i.,* spik.
SCABIES: *n.,* kaskas.
SCALD: *v.t.,* kukim long hat wara.
SCALE: *n.,* skel; *v.t.,* skelim.
SCANDAL: *n.,* samting nogut.
SCARED: *a.,* pret.
SCARF: *n.,* pus.
SCARLET: *a.,* red, redpela.
SCATTER: *v.t.,* hipim nabaut, tromweim nabaut.
SCAVANGE: *v.i.,* mumut; *v.t.,* mumutim.
SCENT: *n.,* (bottled) santa; smel.
SCHEME: *n.,* tink.
SCHOLAR: *n.,* sumatin.
SCHOOL: *n.,* skul. See also SKULANKA.
SCHOOLBOY: *n.,* sumatin, skulboi.
SCHOONER: *n.,* skuna.
SCISSORS: *n.,* sisis.
SCOLD: *v.t.,* krosim.
SCOOP: *v.t.,* sovelim.
SCORCH: *v.t.,* kukim; BE SCORCHED- paiya.
SCRAPE: *v.t.,* skrapim.
SCRATCH: *v.t.,* skrapim.
SCREAM: *v.i.,* singaut; *n.,* singaut.
SCREW: *n.,* skru.
SCREWDRIVER: *n.,* skrudraiwa.
SCRIPTURE: *n.,* baibel, buk tambu.
SCROTUM: *n.,* bol.
SEA: *n.,* solwara.
SEA EAGLE: *n.,* manangunai.
SEAGULL: *n.,* kanai.
SEALING WAX: *n.,* meme.
SEARCH: *v.t.,* painim long; SEARCH FOR- painim.
SEASIDE: *n.,* nambis.
SEASON: *n.,* taim; S.E. SEASON- taim bilong Rai; N.E. SEASON- taim bilong Taleo.
SEAT: *n.,* sia, bet.
SEAWARD: *adv.,* long hap bilong solwara.
SECOND: *n., ord.,* namba tu.
SECRET: *a.,* bilong slip, bilong hait; *n.,* samting bilong hait.
SECRETARY: *n.,* kuskus.
SECRETLY: *adv.,* stil.
SECTION: *n.,* hap.
SECURE: *a.,* pas; *v.t.,* pasim gut.

SEDIMENT: *n.,* meme.
SEDUCE: *v.t.,* pulim.
SEE: *v.t.,* lukim.
SEED: *n.,* pikinini.
SEEDLING: *n.,* kru.
SEEK: *v.t.,* painim; *v.i.,* ask nabaut, painim nabaut.
SEEM, TO: olosem.
SEIZE: *v.t.,* holimpas.
SELECT: *v.t.,* makim.
SELF: *n.,* yet (e.g., mi yet, yu yet).
SELL: *v.t.,* peim.
SEMEN: *n.,* melek.
SEND: *v.t.,* salim; SEND FOR- singaut long.
SENILE: *a.,* lapun.
SENTRY: *n.,* was.
SEPARATE: *a.,* narapela; *v.t.,* opim; lainim wankain na wankain.
SEPTEMBER: *n.,* Septemba.
SERENE: *a.,* klin, klia.
SERGEANT: *n.,* Saitan.
SERMON: *n.,* orovasio.
SERPENT: *n.,* snek.
SERVANT: *n.,* mankimasta, boi.
SETTLE: *v.t.,* stretim.
SEVENTH-DAY ADVENTIST: *prop.n.,* Sevende.
SEVER: *v.t.,* katim.
SEVERAL: *a.,* sampela.
SEVERE: *a.,* hot, strongpela, sakman *(q.v.).*
SEW: *v.t.,* samapim.
SEXUAL INTERCOURSE: *v.i.* & *n.,* puspus; *v.t.,* puspusim, goapim.
SHABBY: *a.,* rabis.
SHADE: *n.,* ples kol.
SHADOW: *n.,* dewel.
SHAKE: *v.i.,* guria, meknais; *v.t.,* sakim; SHAKE HANDS- sikan.
SHALL: *v.,* bai, laik. See Chapter VI.
SHAM: *n.,* giaman.
SHAME: *n.,* sem; BE SHAMED- gat sem.
SHARE: *n.,* hap; *v.t.,* dilim, salim hap.
SHARP: *a.,* sap.
SHARPEN: *v.t.,* sapim.
SHATTER: *v.t.,* brukim olgeta.
SHAVE: *v.i.,* katim gras, sev.
SHE: *pers.pr.,* em.
SHEARS: *n.,* bikpela sisis.

SHED: *n.,* haus, stua.
SHEEP: *n.,* sipsip.
SHEET: *n.,* sitbet; (Naut.) sit, mensit *q.v.*
SHEET IRON: *n.,* kapa.
SHELF: *n.,* tebal, bet.
SHELL: *n.,* (sea) sel, gamsel, skin. See section Fish in classified vocabulary.
    CONCH S.- taul. BAILER S.- gam.
SHELLFISH: *n.,* gamsel.
SHIELD: *n.,* (wooden) plank.
SHILLING: *n.,* siling, mak.
SHIN: *n.,* leg.
SHINE: *v.i.,* lait.
SHIP: *n.,* sip.
SHIRK: *v.t.,* abrusim.
SHIRT: *n.,* siot. A T-shirt is a "singlis".
SHIVER: *v.i.,* guria.
SHOE: *n.,* siu.
SHOOT: *v.t.,* siutim; TARGET SHOOT- siut sewa.
SHOP: *n.,* stua.
SHORE: *n.,* nambis, sua.
SHORT: *a.,* sot, sotpela.
SHOTGUN: *n.,* gan pisin, mambu.
SHOULDER: *n.,* sol.
SHOVE: *v.t.,* siubim.
SHOUT: *v.i.,* singaut.
SHOVEL: *n.,* sovel.
SHOW: *v.t.,* soim.
SHRIMP: *n.,* liklik kindam.
SHROUDS: (Naut.) *n.,* riken.
SHRUB: *n.,* pulpul.
SHUN: *v.t.,* ronewe long ..., klia long ..., abrusim.
SHUT: *v.t.,* pasim.
SHY: *a.,* sem.
SICK: *a.,* sik; SICKNESS- sik.
SIDE: *n.,* hap, hapsait, sait; *anat.,* banis.
SIGN: *n.,* mak.
SILENT: *a.,* nong.
SILK: *n.,* silka.
SILLY: *a.,* kranki, longlong.
SIMILAR: *a.,* olsem, wankain.
SIMPLE: *a.,* samting nating.
SIN: *n.,* pekato.
SINEW: *n.,* rop.

SING: *v.i.,* singsing.
SINGLE: *a.,* wanpela: UNMARRIED- yangpela, skelman.
SINGLET: *n.,* singlis.
SINK: *v.i.,* goraun.
SIP: *v.t.,* traiem.
SISTER: *n.,* sister of a man – sisa; of a woman – brata. See p.39. NUN- sista.
SIT: *v.i.,* sindaun.
SITE: *n.,* ples.
SIXPENCE: *n.,* sikspens, hap mak.
SKELETON: *n.,* bun.
SKIN: *n.,* skin.
SKIRT: *n.,* klos; GRASS SKIRT- pulpul.
SKY: *n.,* antap.
SLACK: *a.,* slek; *v.t.,* slekim.
SLANG: *n.,* tok bokis. See p.115.
SLAP: *v.t.,* slapim.
SLATE: *n.,* tapel.
SLAUGHTER: *n.,* virua. S. A BEAST- kilim.
SLEEP: *v.i.,* slip.
SLEEPY: *a.,* ai i hevi.
SLEEVE: *n.,* han bilong siot (saket, etc.).
SLENDER: *a.,* longpela nating.
SLICE: *n.,* hap; *v.t.,* katim.
SLIGHTLY: *adv.,* liklik.
SLING: *n.,* (ship's) kalabus.
SLIPPER: *n.,* siu.
SLIPPERY: *a.,* wel.
SLIT GONG: *n.,* garamut.
SLOW: *a.,* slo; GO SLOWLY- langsam; *v.i.,* go slo.
SMACK: *v.t.,* paitim, slapim.
SMALL: *a.,* liklik. TOO SMALL- no inap.
SMART: *v.i.,* pait; *a.,* bilas.
SMASH: *v.t.,* brukim olgeta.
SMELL: *v.t.,* smelim; *n.,* smel.
SMILE: *v.i.* and *n.,* lap.
SMOKE: *n.* and *v.i.,* smok; *v.t.,* smokim.
SMOOTH: *a.,* klin tumas, stret; *v.t.,* stretim. SMOOTH WATER- klin wara.
SMOTHER: *v.t.,* pasim win bilong ...
SNAKE: *a.,* snek. CARPET SNAKE- moran.
SNEAK: *v.i.,* stil; *n.,* stilman.
SNOUT: maus, nus.
SO: *adv.,* olsem; *conj.,* orait.

SOAP: *n.*, sop.
SOCK: *n.*, soken.
SODOMY, –IST: aismalang. See fakimas.
SOFA: *n.*, bet.
SOFT: *a.*, melum melum; SOFTLY: *adv.*, isi.
SOIL: *n.*, graun: SOILED- doti.
SOLDER: *n.*, bol, solda; *v.t.*, wokim long bol, soldarim.
SOLDIER: *n.*, soldia.
SOLICITOR: *n.*, masta kot.
SOLID: *a.*, strong.
SOLITARY: *n.* and *adj.adv.*, wanpis.
SOME: *a.*, sampela.
SOMETHING: *n.*, samting.
SOMETIMES: *adv.* sampela taim.
SON: *n.*, pikinini man.
SONG: *n.*, singsing.
SOON: *adv.*, liklik taim.
SOOT: *n.*, sit bilong lam.
SORCERY: *n.*, poisin. Also a term for SORCERER.
SORE: *n.*, sua; *a.*, im i pen.
SORROW: *n.*, sori.
SORRY: *a.*, sori.
SORT: *n.*, wankain, kain.
SOUL: *n.*, dewel.
SOUND: *n.*, meknais, krai; (Naut.) kolim mak.
SOUP: *n.*, sup.
SOUR: *a.*, i pait liklik.
SOURCE: *n.*, as; S. OF RIVER- ai bilong wara.
SOW: *v.t.*, plantim. SOW: *n.*, pik meri.
SPADE: *n.*, sped.
SPANISH: *n.*, Pranis.
SPANNER: *n.*, spana.
SPEAK: *v.i.*, tok, spik.
SPEAR: *n.*, spia.
SPECIES: *n.*, wankain, kain.
SPECTACLES: *n.*, aiglas.
SPEECH: *n.*, tok.
SPELL: *v.t.*, kauntim; *n.*, malira, papait, poisin. See REST.
SPIDER: *n.*, binatang bilong wokim umben, spaida.
SPILL: *v.t.*, kapsaitim; *v.i.*, kapsait.
SPIRIT: *n.*, tambaran, dewel, masalai. *q.v.* HOLY SPIRIT- Dewel Takondo.SPIRITS, METHYLATED: *n.*, spiris.
SPIT: *n.* and *v.i.*, spet; *v.t.*, spetim.

SPLICE: *v.t.,* blaisim.
SPLIT: *v.t.,* brukim longpela.
SPOIL: *v.t.,* bagarapim, mekim nogut, nogutim.
SPOON: *n.,* spun.
SPORT: *n.* and *v.i.,* ple.
SPOUSE: *n.,* marit.
SPRING: *v.i.,* kalap; *n.,* wara i kamap long graun. See SEASON.
SPROUT: *n.,* kru.
SPY: *n.,* stilman; *v.i.,* stil; *v.t.,* stilim.
SQUALL: *n.,* skol.
SQUID: *n.,* tauka.
STAB: *v.t.,* siutim. (Long naip, long spia, etc.)
STAIRS: *n.,* lata.
STALK: *n.,* stik; *v.i.,* stil i go.
STAND: *v.i.,* sanap; *v.t.,* sanapim.
STAND BY: *v.i.,* sambai.
STAR: *n.,* sta.
STARBOARD: (Naut.) *n.,* stiabot.
STARCH: *n.,* stas.
START: *v.i.,* kirap; *v.t.,* kirapim.
STARVE: *v.i.,* dai long hanggre.
STATEMENT: *n.,* tok.
STAY: *v.i.,* stap, sindaun.
STEADFAST: *a.,* strong.
STEAL: *v.t.,* stilim; *v.i.,* stil.
STEEL: *n.,* ain.
STEEP: *a.,* sap.
STEER: *v.i.,* stia.
STEERSMAN: *n.,* stiaman.
STEM: *n.,* stik.
STEPS: *n.,* (house) lata.
STERN: *n.,* as; *a.,* hat. S. OF BOAT- stan.
STICK: *n.,* stik; *v.i.,* pas long ...
STIFF: *a.,* strong.
STING: *v.i.,* pait.
STINGRAY: *n.,* stingre, korvo. MANTA RAY- *(Manta berostis)* epa.
STIR: *v.t.,* tanim, tantanim.
STIRRUP: *n.,* tirap.
STOCKING: *n.,* soken.
STOMACH: *n.,* bel.
STONE: *n.,* ston.
STONY: *a.,* gat ston.
STOP: *v.t.,* mekim dai; *v.i.,* dai pinis; REST, BE AT- stap long ...

STORE: *n.*, stua; WAREHOUSE- bakstua.
STORM: *n.*, bik ren; STORMY WEATHER- taim nogut.
STORY: *n.*, tok kuskus, stori.
STOVE: *n.*, stov.
STRAIGHT: *a.*, stret.
STRAIGHTEN: *v.t.*, mekim stret, stretim.
STRAIN: *v.t.*, taitim.
STRAIT: *n.*, pasis.
STRAP: *n.*, let.
STREAM: *n.*, wara.
STREET: *n.*, rot.
STRENGTH: *n.*, strong.
STRENGTHEN: *v.t.*, mekim strong.
STRETCH: *v.t.*, taitim.
STRICT: *a.*, hat, hatpela.
STRIKE: *v.t.*, paitim; STRIKE VERY HARD- kilim; STRIKE MATCHES- slekim masis.
STRING: *n.*, twain.
STRONG: *a.*, strong.
STUCK: *a.*, pas.
STUDENT: *n.*, sumatin, skulboi.
STUDY: *v.t.*, lainim.
STUMP: *n.*, as.
STUNNED: *a.*, ai raun.
STUPID: *a.*, longlong, nasau.
STURDY: *a.*, strong.
SUAVE: *a.*, gris; also SUAVITY.
SUBMERGE: *v.i.*, go daun.
SUBSEQUENT: *a.*, bilong bihain.
SUBSIDE: *v.i.*, go daun, pinis.
SUBSTITUTE: *n.*, halivim; *v.t.*, senisim.
SUCH: *a.*, olsem.
SUCKLE: *v.t.*, givim susu.
SUDDEN: *a.*, kwik tumas.
SUE: *v.t.*, kotim.
SUET: *n.*, gris.
SUFFICIENT: *a.*, inap.
SUGAR: *n.*, suka.
SUICIDE, COMMIT: mekim nogut skin bilongem, mekim dai em yet.
SUITABLE: *a.*, inap.
SUITCASE: *n.*, paus.
SULKY: *a.*, kros.
SUN: *n.*, san.

SUNDAY: *n.*, Sande.
SUNDOWN: *n.*, san i go daun.
SUNFISH: *n.*, epa *(Manta berostis)*.
SUNRISE: *n.*, tulait, long san i girap.
SUNSET: *n.*, long san i go daun.
SUPERB: *a.*, nambawan tru.
SUPERIOR: *a.*, antap.
SUPERVISE: *v.t.*, bosim.
SUPPER: *n.*, kaikai. Context distinguishes among breakfast, lunch, dinner, etc.
SUPPLIES: *n.*, kago. SUPPLY: *v.t.*, selim.
SUPPOSE: *v.t.*, tingim; I SUPPOSE- aitingk.
SURF: *n.*, si.
SURFACE: *n.*, antap.
SURGEON: *n.*, dokta.
SURLY: *a.*, kros.
SURMISE: *v.t.*, tingim.
SURPASS: *v.t.*, winim.
SURROUND: *v.t.*, banisim.
SURVEYOR: *n.*, masta mak.
SUSPECT: *v.t.*, tingim.
SUSPEND: *v.t.*, hanggimapim.
SWAGGER: *v.i.*, tok bilas.
SWAMP: *n.*, ples melum melum.
SWAP: *v.t.*, senisim.
SWARM: *v.i.*, bung.
SWEAT: *n.*, tuhat.
SWEEP: *v.t.*, brumim.
SWEET: *a.*, swit and switpela.
SWEET POTATO: *n.*, kaukau.
SWELL: *v.i.*, solap.
SWIFT: *a.*, kwik.
SWIM: *v.t.* and *i.*, siubim wara, swim. Often suim and suimim.
SWINDLE: *v.t.*, giamanim.
SWORD: *n.*, naip.
SYMBOL: *n.*, mak.
SYMPATHIZE: *v.i.*, sori long.
SYSTEM: *n.*, pasin.

TABLE: *n.*, tebal.
TABOO: *n.*, tambu.
TACK: *n.*, liklik nil. Boats: TACK CLOSE TO THE WIND- kipap.
TAIL: *n.*, tel.

TAKE: *v.t.,* kisim.
TAKE AWAY: *v.t.,* tekewe, kisim i go.
TALC: *n.,* kampang; TALCUM POWDER- kampang smel.
TALE: *n.,* tok kuskus, stori.
TALK: *v.i.* and *n.,* tok, toktok.
TALL: *a.,* longpela.
TALLOW: *n.,* gris.
TALON: *n.,* kapa, nil.
TANGLED: *a.,* faulnabaut.
TANK: *n.,* tank.
TAP: *n.,* kok bilong tank.
TAR: *n.,* kolta.
TARO: *n.,* taro.
TARDY: *a.,* slo; BE TARDY- langsam.
TARGET: *n.,* sewa, tagis.
TARPAULIN: *n.,* tapulit.
TASK: *n.,* wok.
TASTE: *v.t.,* traiem.
TAUNT: *v.t.,* tok bilas long.
TAX: *n.,* takis; PAY TAX- tromwe takis.
TEA: *n.,* ti; lip ti (leaves).
TEACH: *v.t.,* lainim, skulim.
TEACHER: *n.,* tisa.
TEAM: *n.,* lain.
TEAPOT: *n,.* tipot.
TEAR: *v.t.,* brukim; *n.,* hul.
TEAR: *n.,* wara bilong ai.
TEAT: *n.,* ai bilong susu.
TEETH: *n.,* tis.
TELEPHONE: *n.,* talipon; *v.t.,* talipon long.
TELL: *v.t.,* tokim.
TEMPT: *v.t.,* grisim, traiem.
TENDON: *n.,* rop.
TENT: *n.,* haus sel.
TENTFLY: *n.,* sel.
TEPID: *a.,* hat liklik.
TERMINATE: *v.t.,* pinisim.
TERMITE: *n.,* anis bilong kaikai diwai.
TERRIFIED: *a.,* pret tumas.
TEST: *v.t.,* traiem.
TESTICLE: *n.,* kiau.
TETHER: *v.t.,* pasim.
THANKS: tenkyu.

THAT: *dem.a.,* em (long hap).
THATCH: *n.,* kunai; marota; kanda (rattan leaves).
THEATRE: *n.,* haus piksa.
THEIR: *poss.pro.,* bilongen.
THEM: *pers.pr.,* em, ol.
THEMSELVES: *pers.pr.,* em yet.
THEN: *adv.,* bipo, long taim hia; *conj.,* nau.
THERE: *adv.,* long hap; THERE IS ... i gat ...
THEREFORE: *conj.,* orait.
THESE: *dem.a.,* em hia.
THEY: *pers.pr.,* em, em ol.
THICK: *a.,* bikpela, sotpela.
THIEF: *n.,* stilman.
THIEVE: *v.t.,* stilim.
THIGH: *n.,* sangana.
THIN: *a.,* liklik, longpela.
THING: *n.,* samting.
THINK: *v.i.,* tingktingk (tingting); *v.t.,* tingkim (tingim).
THIRSTY: *a.,* nek i drai.
THIS: *dem.a.,* hia, em ... hia, dispela. See grammar p.17.
THORN: *n.,* nil.
THOSE: *dem.a.,* em (long hap).
THOUGHT: *n.,* tingk, tingktingk.
THOUGHTLESS: *a.,* nogat tingktingk.
THRASH: *v.t.,* hamarim, paitim.
THREAD: *n.,* tret.
THREEPENCE: *n.,* tripens.
THRICE: *num.adv.,* tritaim.
THROAT: *n.,* nek.
THROUGH: *prep.,* long, nisait long ...
THROW: *v.t.,* tromwe.
THRUST: *v.t.,* siubim.
THUMB: *n.,* pinga.
THUNDER: *v.i.,* klaut i pairap.
THURSDAY: *n.,* Fonde.
THUS: *adv.,* olsem.
TIDE: *n.,* haiwara. (Tait is a current). LOW TIDE- draiwara.
TIDY: *a.,* klin, stret.
TIE: *v.t.,* pasim; *n.,* nektai.
TIGHT: *a.,* tait, strong.
TIGHTEN: *v.t.,* taitim.
TILLER: *n.,* stia.
TIMBER: *n.,* diwai, plangk.

TIME: *n.*, taim; WHAT IS THE TIME- haumas klok?
TIMID: *a.*, pret.
TIN: *n.*, tin. TIN-OPENER- optin.
TIP: *n.*, ai.
TITLE: *n.*, nem.
TO: *prep.*, long.
TOAD: *n.*, dokorok (em i blak).
TOADFISH: *n.*, bikbel, bokis.
TOAST: *n.*, tos.
TOBACCO: *n.*, tabak; FINE-CUT- kepstan; LEAF- brus.
TODAY: *n.*, tude.
TOE: *n.*, pinga bilong lek. TOENAIL- kapa.
TOGETHER: *adv.*, wantaim.
TOIL: *n.* and *v.i.*, hatwok.
TOILET: *n.*, haus pekpek, smolhaus.
TOKEN: *n.*, mak.
TOMAHAWK: *n.*, tomiok.
TOMATO: *n.*, tumato.
TOMORROW: *n.*, tumora.
TONGUE: *n.*, tang.
TOO: *adv.*, tu; *rel.adv.*, tumas.
TOOTH: *n.*, tis.
TOP: *n.*, antap.
TORCH: *n.*, electric torch – siutlam; palm frond torch – bombom.
TORRENT: *n.*, tait.
TORTOISE: *n.*, liklik torasel.
TORTUOUS: *a.*, sneknabaut.
TOSS: *v.t.*, tromwe.
TOTAL: *a.*, olgeta.
TOTEM: *n.*, pisin.
TOUCH: *v.t.*, holim, traiem.
TOUGH: *a.*, strong.
TOUR: *v.t.*, raun long ...
TOW: *v.t.*, pulim.
TOWARD: *prep.*, long, hapigo long ...
TOWEL: *n.*, taul.
TOWN: *n.*, ples, tesin.
TRACK: *n.*, rot. See TRAIL.
TRACT: *n.*, hap.
TRADE: *n.*, bisnis.
TRAIL: *n.*, lek; *v.t.*, bihainim lek.
TRAIN: *v.t.*, skulim.
TRANSFER: *v.t.*, senisim i go.

TRANSLATE: *v.t.,* tanim.
TRANSPARENT: *a.,* klia.
TRAVEL: *v.t.,* go, gokambaut.
TRAY: *n.,* plank.
TREE: *n.,* diwai.
TREMBLE: *v.i.,* guria.
TREMOR: *n.,* guria.
TRENCH: *n.,* barat. A short trench is a "hul".
TREPANG: *n.,* pislama.
TREVALLY: *n.,* langul.
TRICK: *n.,* giaman; *v.t.,* giamanim.
TRIFLE: *n.,* samting nating.
TRIM: *a.,* stret; klin.
TRINITY, HOLY: *prop.n.,* Trinitas Takondo.
TRIP OVER: *v.t.,* kronggutim.
TROCUS: *n.,* lalai.
TROUBLE: *n.,* trabel.
TROUSERS: *n.,* trausis.
TRUCK: *n.,* lori, trak.
TRUE: *a.,* tru; stret (measurements, levels, etc.).
TRUMPET: *n.,* biugil.
TRUNK: *n.,* bokis. There is no specific word for "tree trunk", but all the rest of the tree is named – skin (bark), rop (roots), han (branches), lip (leaves), blut (sap), etc., depending on the tree.
TRUTH: *n.,* tok i tru.
TRY: *v.t.,* traiem; *v.i.,* mekim nating.
TUB: *n.,* tab.
TUBE: *n.,* paip.
TUESDAY: *n.,* Tunde.
TUMBLE: *v.i.,* pudaon.
TUNA: *n.,* atun.
TUNIC: *n.,* saket.
TUNNY: *n.,* (fish) atun.
TURKEY: *n.,* pipi.
TURN: *v.t.,* tanim; *v.i.,* baut. MY TURN- mi nau.
TURTLE: *n.,* torasel.
TWICE: *adv.,* tupelataim, tutaim.
TWILIGHT: *n.,* klosap tudak.
TWIN: *n.,* proman; see twins below.
TWINE: *n.,* twain.
TWINS: *n.,* sangsangana.
TWIST: *v.t.,* tantanim. TWISTED- kronggut.
TWO: *num.a.,* tupela; *card.n.,* tu.

TYRANT: *n.,* sakman.

UDDER: *n.,* susu.
ULCER: *a.,* strongpela sua.
UMBRELLA: *n.,* ambrela.
UNABLE: *a.,* noken.
UNASKED: *adv.,* nating.
UNBIND: *v.t.,* lusim.
UNCLE: *n.,* smolpapa, papa; MATERNAL UNCLE- kandere.
UNCONSCIOUS, BE: dai
UNCOOKED: *a.,* no dan, amat.
UNDER: *prep.,* ananit long.
UNDERSTAND: *v.i.* and *v.t.,* save.
UNDRESS: *v.i.,* lusim klos, trausis, siot, etc.
UNEMPLOYED: *a.,* no gat wok.
UNFIT: *a.,* no inap.
UNFORTUNATE: *a.,* taronggu. See kalopa.
UNHAPPY: *a.,* taronggu.
UNIQUE: *a.,* narakain.
UNITE: *v.t.,* see JOIN; *v.i.,* bung, bung wantaim.
UNLESS: *conj.,* sapos ... no. See p.23.
UNLOAD: *v.t.,* tekewe kago.
UNLUCKY: *n.,* taronggu.
UNOCCUPIED: *n.,* nating.
UNPLEASANT: *a.,* nogut.
UNSUITABLE: *a.,* no inap.
UNTIE: *v.t.,* lusim. See p.95.
UNTIL: *prep.,* inap long.
UNWILLING: *a.,* no laik.
UPON: *prep.,* long, antap long.
UPRIGHT: *a.,* stret.
UPWARDS: *adv.,* i go antap.
URGE: *v.t.,* pulim, kirapim.
URINE: *n.,* pispis. URINATE- pispis.
US: *pers.pr.,* yumi, mipela. See grammar.
USE: *v.t.,* wok long ...; *n.,* bilong wonem wok.
USUAL: *a.,* olsem (after the noun).

VACANT: *a.,* nogat samting, nating.
VACATION: *n.,* limlimbu.
VAGINA: *n.,* bokis.
VALET: *n.,* mankimasta.
VALLEY: *n.,* barat.
VANISH: *v.i.,* see DISAPPEAR.

VAPOUR: *n.*, smok.
VARIABLE: *a.*, bilong senisnabaut.
VARIOUS: *a.*, olkain, planti kain.
VEGETABLE: *n.*, see Classified Vocabulary.
VEIN: *n.*, rop.
VENEER: *n.*, skin.
VERANDAH: *n.*, branda, banis.
VERTIGO: *n.*, ai i raun.
VERY: *adv.*, tumas.
VESSEL: *n.*, sip.
VETERAN: *a.*, bilong longtaim.
VIBRATE: *v.i.*, guria: *v.t.*, sekim.
VICINITY, IN THE: klostu long.
VICTORY: *n.*, win.
VIE: *v.i.*, resis.
VIGIL: *n.*, was.
VILE: *a.*, nogut tru.
VILLAGE: *n.*, ples.
VILLAIN: *n.*, man nogut.
VINE: *n.*, rop. See KRAKON and KANDA.
VIPER: *n.*, snek.
VIRILE: *a.*, strong.
VIRILITY: *n.*, strong.
VISCERA: *n.*, bel.
VISIT: *v.t.*, limlimbu long, go lukim.
VITAL: *a.*, samting tru.
VOICE: *n.*, nek.
VOID: *a.*, (void of) nogat.
VOMIT: *v.i.*, and *n.*, traut.
VULVA: *n.*, kan.

WADDING: *n.*, kapuk.
WAGES: *n.*, pe.
WAIL: *v.i.*, krai.
WAIT: *v.i.*, wet; **WAIT FOR-** wetim.
WAKE: *v.i.*, kirap; *v.t.*, kirapim.
WALK: *v.i.*, wokabaut.
WALL: *n.*, banis.
WALLABY: *n.*, sikau.
WALLET: *n.*, paus.
WALNUT: *n.*, (tree) laup.
WANDER: *v.i.*, gokambaut.
WANT: *v.t.*, laikim; *aux.*, laik.
WAR: *n.*, pait, wor.

WAREHOUSE: *n.*, bakstua.
WARSHIP: *n.*, manuwa.
WART: *n.*, tono – especially *plantar*.
WARY: *a.*, pret.
WASH: *v.t.*, wasim; *v.i.*, waswas; *n.*, waswas.
WASP: *n.*, binatang bilong pait.
WATCH: *n.*, klok.
WATCH: *v.i.*, was; *v.t.*, was long; *n.*, was.
WATCHMAN: *n.*, was.
WATER: *n.*, wara. WATER RACE- barat (irrigation).
WATERCRESS: *n.*, kangko.
WATERMELON: *n.*, melen.
WAVE: *n.*, si.
WAX: *n.*, meme.
WAY: *n.*, rot; pasin.
WE: *pers.pr.*, yumi, mipela. See p.16.
WEAK: *a.*, no strong, hanggre.
WEAR: *v.t.*, putim.
WEARY: *a.*, dai long slip.
WEBBING: *n.*, kandis.
WEDDING: *n.*, marit.
WEDNESDAY: *n.*, Trinde.
WEED: *n.*, pipia gras.
WEEK: *n.*, wik.
WEEP: *v.i.*, kraikrai.
WEIGH: *v.t.*, skelim.
WELL: *adv.*, gut; *n.*, hul bilong wara.
WELL-NIGH: *adv.*, klosap.
WEST: *adv.*, long hap bilong san i go daun.
WET: *a.*, kol, gat wara.
WHACK HO! *excl.*, hotpela!
WHALE: *n.*, bikpela pis.
WHALEBOAT: *n.*, lanis.
WHARF: *n.*, bris.
WHAT?: *interrog.p.*, wonem. See Grammar.
WHEATMEAL: *n.*, plaua.
WHEEL: *n.*, wilwil.
WHEELBARROW: *n.*, wilka, supkar.
WHEN?: long wonem taim? Wataim: *adv.*, long taim.
WHENCE?: we?
WHERE?: we? westap?
WHICH: *interrog.pr.*, wonem.
WHILE: *adv.*, long taim; *n.*, liklik taim.

WHIM: *n.,* wisis.
WHISKERS: *n.,* mausgras.
WHISKY: *n.,* wiski.
WHISTLE: *n.* and *v.i.,* wisil.
WHITE: *a.,* wait, waitpela.
WHITEBAIT: *n.,* aina, ainanga.
WHITE MAN: *n.,* waitman.
WHITEWASH: *n.,* kampang.
WHO: *interrog.* or *rel.pro.,* husat, wonem man.
WHOLE: *a.,* olgeta.
WHOM: *rel.pr.,* husat.
WHOSE: *poss.pr.,* bilong husat?
WHY: *adv.,* bilong wonem? wasamara? watpo? hausat?
WICK: *n.,* wik.
WIDE: *a.,* brait, braitpela.
WIFE: *n.,* meri bilong ..., misis bilong ...; but "waif" is emerging.
WILD: *a.,* wail, e.g., wail paul, wail pik.
WILL: *aux.v.,* see Chapter VI.
WILLING: *a.,* orait long.
WIN: *v.i.,* win.
WINCH: *a.,* winis.
WIND: *n.,* win; S.E. WIND- Rai; N.W. WIND- Tolo; FOLLOWING WIND- prauwin.
WIND: *v.t.,* tanim; WINDING: *a.,* sneknabaut.
WINDLASS: *n.,* winis.
WINDOW: *n.,* pindua.
WINDPIPE: *n.,* paip bilong nek.
WING: *n.,* wing, han.
WIPE: *v.t.,* klinim, rapim.
WIRE: *n.,* waia.
WIRELESS: *n.,* wailis.
WISH: *v.i.,* laik. Also noun.
WITH: *prep.,* wantaim long.
WITHIN: *prep.,* nisait long, insait.
WITHOUT: *adv.,* aratsaet; *prep.,* nogat. See p.99, Nating.
WOMAN: *n.,* (native) meri; WHITE WOMEN- misis. "Woman" now coming into use.
WOMB: *n.,* bel.
WOO: *v.t.,* hambag long ..., gris long.
WOOD: *n.,* diwai.
WOOL: *n.,* gras; COTTON WOOL- kepok.
WORD: *n.,* tok.
WORK: *n.* and *v.i.,* wok; *v.t.,* wokim.

WORKER: *n.,* wokman, wokboi.
WORLD: *n.,* graun bilong yumi. (This also means "our acres".)
WORM: *n.,* liklik snek.
WORRY: *n.* and *v.,* tingk; WORRY ABOUT IT- tingkim.
WORTHLESS: *a.,* rabis.
WOUND: *v.t.,* bonim (long bol), katim; *n.,* sua.
WRANGLE: *v.i.,* kros.
WRAP: *v.t.,* karamapim, latapim.
WRATH: *n.,* kros.
WRECK: *v.t.,* bagarapim; BE WRECKED- bagarap.
WRIST: *n.,* skru (bilong han); WRISTWATCH- hanwas.
WRITE: *v.i.,* rait; *v.t.,* raitim.
WRONG: *n.,* rong; *a.,* no stret, kranki.
WRYNECK: *n.,* nek kronggut.

YACHT: *n.,* sip, skuna.
YAM: *n.,* yam, mami – different varieties of discorea.
YARD: *n.,* banis.
YAWS: *n.,* tambilua.
YEAR: *n.,* yiar.
YEARN: *v.i.,* sotwin (long), dai (long).
YEAST: *n.,* yis.
YELL: *v.i.,* singaut.
YELLOW: *a.,* yelo, yelopela.
YES: *adv.,* yesa, yes.
YESTERDAY: *adv.,* asade.
YET: *adv.,* yet.
YOU: *pron.,* yu (sing), yupela (pl.).
YOUNG: *a.,* yangpela.
YOUR: *poss.pr.,* bilong yu, bilong yupela.
YOURSELF: *pron.,* yu yet.
YOUTH: *n.,* manki.

ZEALOUS: *a.,* strong, hat.
ZERO: *n.,* nating.
ZEST: have zest for – laikim tumas long ...
ZIGZAG: *a.,* nabaut nabaut, snek nabaut.
ZINC: *n.,* kapa.
ZIPPER: *n.,* pulsen.
ZONE: *n.,* hap.
ZOOM: *v.i.,* siut i go.